CHOOSE YOUR THOUGHTS, CHANGE YOUR LIFE

How to harness the power of your thinking

JANE DUNCAN

1997

Choose your thoughts, change your life
How to harness the power of your thinking

Copyright ©1997 Jane Duncan

All rights reserved. No part of this book may be reproduced, stored in a retrieval system, or transmitted, in any form or by any means, electronic, mechanical, photocopying, recording or otherwise, except for short extracts for quotation or review, without the prior permission of the publishers.

Published in England by
Living Well Publications, 27 Earl Street, Oxford OX2 0JA
Telephone 07050 074875 *(mobile phone rates)*

ISBN 0-9531380-0-3

This book is sold subject to the condition that it shall not, by way of trade or otherwise, be lent, re-sold, hired out, or otherwise circulated without the publisher's prior consent in any form of binding or cover other than that in which it is published and without a similar condition including this condition being imposed on the subsequent purchaser.

Printed by The Guernsey Press
Cover and text design Will Shaman

Set in 9 on 16pt Americana and Monotype Gill Sans

Dedication

To the many people over the years who have asked me questions such as 'How do affirmations actually work?', 'How do I practice them?' and 'Am I doing it right?', I hope this book will provide answers, for them, and for those who may ask in the future.

Acknowledgments

Every year I spend some time in Scotland at our cottage by the sea which my grandfather built in 1947. Last year, while there, it became clear to me that it was the right time to write this book, and for this reason I am grateful to both my grandfather and the place itself, for it is there that I am able often to realise my dreams.

Kate Howlett was instrumental in the shaping of this book, particularly giving advice and editorial comments. My parents willingly read the manuscript, and were supportive and encouraging, as always, as were my brother Simon and his wife Cath. Seren did a great job of editing, as did Anna of proofing. Will's design work is much appreciated, along with his cheerfulness!

I am also grateful to Debbie and Eddie Shapiro and Robert and Miranda Holden, who have been encouraging and helpful in many practical ways, but also as friends with whom we can relax. Thank you to my clients and those participating in workshops, who have taught me more than they will ever know, and to Judith who continues to provide a space where I am nourished.

Without Louise Hay, affirmations would not have become such an important part of my life. Thank you, Louise, for sharing yourself with me, and for your continuous support over the years.

The importance of learning from our negative thoughts, as outlined here, comes almost entirely from the fascinating discussions on this topic I have had with my husband, Philip Rogers. For this, and for his willingness to read and re-read the manuscript, I am grateful.

How to use this book

This book is designed to be used as a practical manual to help you actually make changes in your life. Many of the ideas, especially if you are new to them, can be quite challenging and time may be needed to reflect and discover your ideas and beliefs about a particular topic, so be sure to take the amount of time that is right for you. You will find using a personal journal useful as an accompaniment to this book, not only for recording your responses to particular exercises, but also so that you can write down any feelings and thoughts that arise for you as you progress – and of course, in which you can write affirmations! Most important, however, is that you treat yourself on this journey with kindness and compassion.

NOTE

All examples in this book are based on real situations and real people. However, for reasons of confidentiality, all names and identifying details have been changed.

Contents

Introduction 13

Chapter One: Principles behind positive affirmation 19

positive affirmations – a definition
the truth of a positive statement
choosing to believe
the energy in our actions
thoughts also have energy
looking at things with a different perspective
self-fulfilling prophecies
the polarities of positive and negative
the common denominator
anything is possible

Chapter Two: How do positive affirmations work? 29

your internal boxes and filing system
familiarity
what are some of your negative boxes?
where do our files and boxes come from?
our childhood patterns
getting out of a negative box

Chapter Three: Challenges to thinking positively 37

worrying about what's in your box
objections to positive statements
judging your negative thoughts
if things seem to be getting worse
fear of change

Chapter Four: Discovering negative beliefs 43

    negative family sayings
    a message for parents
    we do the best we can, given what we know
    negative things you say now
    storylines, dramas and themes
    identifying your own storylines, dramas and themes

Chapter Five: Using affirmations 65

    adding to your positive boxes and files
    affirming life itself
    guidelines to creating affirmations
    compiling an affirmation step by step
    practising counteracting negative statements with
        positive affirmations
    changing your negative thoughts and beliefs into
        positive ones

Chapter Six: Practising Your Affirmations 79

    writing them down
    making affirmative notices
    using a mirror
    the power of imagery
    making your own tape
    affirming while exercising
    saying affirmations with a partner
    the three P's: practise
                      persistence
                      patience
    choosing to be great

Chapter Seven: What you feel, you can heal 93

   getting to know your feelings
   anger
   sadness
   fear
   apathy
   happiness
   being in charge of your feelings
   separating past feelings from present
   embracing and connecting with your younger self

Conclusion 111

Appendix A: Living Well 113

Appendix B: Vocabulary of feelings 115

Appendix C: Some suggested further reading 119

Appendix D: Examples of affirmative notices 123

INTRODUCTION

Observing the way I think and using affirmations have been a part of my life for a long time now. However, over the years as I have grown and changed myself, so too has the way I have used affirmations. I first discovered them through reading Louise Hay and Shakti Gawain and, although the ideas presented in their books were not new to me, using affirmations to change my thinking patterns was. I began to recite them over and over, wanting to discover whether, by changing my thoughts, my life would also change. Unlike many examples I had read, nothing much happened, and I gave up feeling rather disillusioned and blaming myself for not being 'good enough' or 'disciplined enough' to change my thoughts and behaviour. After all, if other people could do it, why couldn't I? I concluded that there had to be something wrong with me.

I remember travelling in India, having made vague plans to meet up with someone later on in Bali. I was hoping to receive a letter from him, and recited over and over, each day 'Today I receive a letter from Paul'. The letter never came, and I felt more and more depressed, despite being in Goa, a beautiful and interesting place. Meanwhile I continued to write in my journal, doing my best to understand my moods, feelings and thoughts, and still feeling somehow that I was failing in some way.

The following year, despite my discouraging start in

using affirmations, I decided to attend what was to be Louise Hay's last training course in America; I was still interested in developing my thoughts by using affirmations, but I needed more help. Getting more practise in the skill of catching my thoughts, and changing them in the presence of others doing the same, was a welcome boost to my self-confidence and motivation.

I began using affirmations in earnest, particularly in the area of my relationships, and about my continuing problem with compulsive eating. I had managed some time previously to stop actually being bulimic, but the obsession to eat was still with me, particularly when under stress. Although at first I did not really believe my affirmations, I had faith that it was possible to make changes in my life by using them, and the fact that saying positive things was something that I could do actively, every day, was a relief – at least I knew I was doing something towards changing my life. Slowly, through challenging my existing beliefs by using positive affirmations, I began to consider new ideas: that I did deserve a loving and supportive relationship; that I was a worthy enough person to take up space in this world, and that I was lovable. I didn't believe these ideas at first – I believed (and had constantly tried to prove to myself) that relationships were not for me, that I didn't deserve any space on the earth, and that I certainly was not lovable. However, I began to explore why I had these negative thoughts, and continued, on and off, to challenge my existing view of myself with positive affirmations.

At this point I really had to trust, because although I could sense that I was changing inside, my circumstances were not changing. I was still only attracted to men who were unavailable for a committed relationship; I still binged on chocolate and overate often, and none of this behaviour helped to make me feel lovable, or even to like myself.

Returning to England, I committed myself to changing these patterns. Still using affirmations, I also joined Overeaters Anonymous. I started to receive counselling, and joined a bioenergetics group (a kind of movement therapy). I learnt to listen to feelings that I had been trying to suppress for years and began to express them instead. As I supported myself in this way, the need to eat compulsively slowly receded, and then, within the next six months I met a (suitable!) man who is now my husband. I had entered a new stage in my life, which brought its own challenges (as life does), but now I had forms of support that were very practical and useful to me.

Now I look back and can understand much more about the process I went through during that time. For instance, while I was in India, waiting for the letter to come, I believed that I was responsible for everything in my life, both the cause and the effect. This idea had gone a long way to making me feel safe at the time and feel that I could control events around me; but I discovered that it was very hard to take on board this concept without also then blaming myself for events that happened and which I did not like, or when things went wrong. Hence my feeling of failure when the letter did not arrive. I concluded that there had to be something wrong with me, or something wrong with the way I was practising my affirmations. Now I see that what I was trying to do with that affirmation was to control circumstances – and I was doing this because I was frightened. I was unable to consider what I now believe – that I was not responsible *for* everything, but that I could choose how I wanted to *respond to* all that happened around me. Fairly soon after my India trip I began reflecting further on this idea of *responding to*, rather than *being responsible for*, and I let go of a lot of self-inflicted pressure. Some things are just unexplainable; there is a mystery to life that is valid in its own right. However, what we do have control over is how we react or respond to life – that is within our capacity to change. As Debbie Shapiro once said 'You can't change the direction of the wind, but you can change the sails'.

Now I tend to use affirmations which are less specific about a particular event happening, and I am more interested in the reasons why the result of the affirmation is not happening in my life. It is these reasons that get in the way of the affirmation being true. So, for instance, in India I might have addressed the idea of *why* I so badly needed to receive a letter from this boyfriend, and affirmed instead that I would meet the right people at the right time.

So, while reading this book, be open to affirmations as a process. As you do this work, also prepare yourself to accept what you say you want when it happens! You will be changing as you use affirmations, and so too will your affirmations. Go at your own pace and enjoy your journey!

Chapter One

Principles behind positive affirmation

Positive affirmations

Many of our thoughts are affirmations without our even realising it, whether they are positive or negative. An affirmation is something you state strongly as if it were true, whether or not you believe it. It is something we say 'Yes' to, as opposed to 'No'. We put our backing behind it, stating strongly that this is what we believe, or want to believe. For instance, when someone moans, it is a negative affirmation, whereas praise and appreciation are positive ones.

The truth of a positive statement

Often when we start to use positive affirmations which are in some way the opposite to what we've always thought or felt, our immediate reaction is that it simply isn't true. Whether something is actually true or not depends to a large extent on the way you look at things. This doesn't necessarily mean that if it is raining outside and you start saying 'it is sunny now' over and over again that the weather will actually change, but it does mean that *you can choose how you respond* to the fact that it is raining. *You* choose, no-one else, whether the rain is going to ruin your day, or whether you are going to have a good day despite the weather.

Choosing to believe

We *can* choose what we believe – and what we believe is the backbone of how we live our lives. Just as our natural backbone, our spine, supports the rest of our physical body, so our beliefs support our mental, spiritual and emotional body. Working with positive affirmations will help you to discover exactly what you believe, and enable you to begin to change unsupportive beliefs.

The energy in our actions

You may be familiar with the concept that the world, both physical and non-physical, is in fact made up of differing densities of energy. For instance, a rock is a very permanent object, made up of dense energy, denser, say, than the leaf of a tree. Scientists are discovering that what they had originally perceived as 'matter' is in fact a composition of different densities of energy.

In our own bodies we can see that all this energy is interrelated. If we sprain our ankle, we will favour that ankle as we gingerly walk for the next few days, redistributing our energy, and letting our opposite leg and hip take the strain. Each small movement in the body affects the rest of our body in some way or another, maybe so minutely we don't even notice it. This is the view of holistic medicine, where practitioners consider the whole body, rather than just the

Principles behind positive affirmation

part that is displaying the symptom of illness. More and more conventional medical doctors are now willing to acknowledge that the human body needs to be seen as a whole system, i.e. holistically.

The same theory applies in how we live our daily lives. Our actions and the energy associated with them have a far-reaching effect on ourselves and other people.

> Tom, whose wife recently died, wakes up late; he has to get his two children up, breakfasted and out to school within twenty minutes, before going to work himself. He leaps out of bed, shouting to the children to get up. His panicking energy affects the children in different ways: the eldest, Hannah, becomes alarmed herself, and starts to worry about what will happen if she is late; Lucy, the youngest, responds to Tom's panicking shouting by wanting to snuggle under her duvet even more. Hannah becomes irritated with Lucy, and pulls her duvet off. Both girls are angry with their Dad for not hearing his alarm and waking up late; and are missing their Mum's organising presence. Tom is angry with himself; with the girls for not cooperating; and with his late wife, for not being there. All three eventually get in the car, but arrive late at school. Hannah is agitated at school because she missed part of her first lesson, and is worrying; Lucy takes an 'I don't care' attitude, suppressing the feeling that she really does; and Tom misses his first meeting of the morning, which has meant his assistant doing extra work on his behalf. He begins to feel guilty on top of everything else.

I'm sure that this scene or a similar one is familiar to many of you; it is a simple example of how our actions and energy affect others around us. We could imagine this scenario in a different way, where the same situation is dealt with differently:

> Tom wakes up late. Initially panicking as he jumps out of bed, he reminds himself in the bathroom that the world is not going to fall apart if he and his girls are late for once. Breathing more deeply to help keep himself calm, he wakes the girls and lets them know that they will be going to school late that day; he then phones both the school and his office to let them know. He realises there will be consequences, particularly at his workplace, but feels good that he has managed the situation well. The girls pick up on his mood, and although not entirely happy that they will be late, are pleased that it has been taken care of and that they won't be reprimanded at school.

Thoughts also have energy

Even without any action taken as a result of a thought, we still emanate energy. Other people can feel this; you may know someone who usually is a joy to be around. They often sound cheerful, enjoy how they live their lives, and find positive aspects even in challenging situations. Their own pleasure in life spills over, and those around them benefit too. But you may also have had the experience of being around someone who is in a bad mood – their body language alone affects everyone around them. They are likely to be thinking (maybe unconsciously) black thoughts: blaming someone for their predicament; being self-critical; criticising others; feeling unworthy; wanting to punish someone or something. The whole atmosphere around

Principles behind positive affirmation

this person can become very unpleasant, and often people will want to drift away or try to ignore them. Others will be drawn to that person, wanting to help them out of their predicament, or drawn to them out of empathy.

What we think affects ourselves, too. When we criticise ourselves or others, it is impossible to feel good.

> Jenny, a single career-woman, woke up feeling grumpy. She had had a disturbed night, and was not looking forward to a business meeting she had later that day. Still feeling out of sorts, she was unhappy upon opening her post to discover a letter from the bank, informing her that she was overdrawn. She immediately felt angry with the bank, and then with herself for not monitoring her account better. She set off for work, continuing to blame herself. Arriving at work, she realised she had double-booked herself and would not be able to attend her meeting. By this time she was thinking it was going to be 'one of those days;' and she began to expect everything to go wrong. Jenny's day continued along the same lines, with her consistently negative thinking taking her further and further down a spiral. By the time it came to five o'clock, she decided she'd better stay on in the office, to make up for her earlier incompetency (as she saw it). Eventually at 7pm she decided to leave, lacking confidence, and with feelings of stress which throughout the day had spread, resulting in her feeling a failure. To cap it all, arriving home, she had forgotten to buy milk and was unable to have a cup of tea. She felt terrible – bad-tempered, lonely and full of tension. Her day had been a manifestation of her self-critical thoughts. There had been no room for allowing herself to make mistakes; she was unable to meet her own high standards, and therefore considered herself a failure.

Criticising ourselves usually will mean that we are putting ourselves down in some way, and it takes practice to realise when we are doing it. If Jenny had been able to notice when she was criticising herself during her day, she would have had the choice to interrupt that pattern and to begin to think more positively, thereby stopping the seemingly inevitable downward spiral.

Looking at things with a different perspective

Imagine looking at a pint glass with half a pint of water in it. Would you say there was a half-full glass or a half-empty glass in front of you? As a generalisation, those of us who tend to see the glass half full will be more likely to see the positive side of a situation, while those who see a half-empty glass will tend to see life more negatively. Given this, of course, we all have times when we can only see the gloomy side of things – and this is quite normal. It is when a gloomy or depressing attitude begins to take us over that we may then start to feel out of control of our lives.

> When I first came to London, in my early twenties, before I'd even heard of affirmations, I used to play mind games on the walk to work through the West End by looking at all the awful things about London – the dirt, pollution, noise, crowds, etc. Then I would switch and appreciate all the wonderful things – the trees amongst the buildings, the architecture, the variety of shops, the fact that people from all over the world came to visit this city in which I was privileged enough to live. This game always worked to make me feel good about my self

and my surroundings. I was choosing to see the glass half full instead of half empty.

Self-fulfilling prophecies

Every time you think or feel something negative about yourself, you contribute to your negative beliefs about yourself – you are giving yourself another message that you are not OK. The more you do this, the more you are likely to find yourself behaving according to that negative judgment. For instance, if you frequently feel you have failed, and then berate yourself for that, you will perpetuate your idea of yourself as a failure, especially if you have been programmed to think of yourself that way, maybe from as far back as early childhood. A self-fulfilling prophecy has come into play, convincing yourself you really are a failure. Self-fulfilling prophecies can work the other way round too though – so we may as well use this principle to support ourselves, rather than have it be detrimental to us.

The polarities of positive and negative

We cannot have the positive without the negative. They exist at opposite ends of a continuum, and consequently have a relationship to each other, just as happiness and sadness exist in relation to each other, or giving and receiving. One cannot exist without the other, nor is it supposed to. What we can do with unwanted thoughts and feelings is to understand and experience the messages and insights they are bringing us, thereby enabling us to let go of them and to move further along the continuum towards the more positive end. Don't be surprised by the extent of negative thinking that may occur when you start consciously to change your negative thoughts to positive ones – learn to appreciate the fact that you've noticed your negative thoughts, and take advantage of the opportunity to change them.

So, for every positive thought we have that we don't believe, we will probably have many more negative thoughts justifying what we do believe. When we are aware of the negative thoughts, we realise clearly what our beliefs are about ourselves.

> Penny had attended a workshop because she recognised her self-esteem was very low and she wanted to explore what she could do to change this. Half way through she reacted strongly when I stated the affirmation 'You deserve the best in life'. She disagreed and reeled off a long list of reasons about why she didn't deserve the best -
>
> 'I'm not good enough to deserve anything, let alone the best'
>
> 'I've behaved too badly in my life to deserve anything'
>
> 'Why should I get the best and not someone else?'

Because others in the group had reacted differently to this affirmation, Penny was able to consider that her ideas were clearly not supporting her, and that she could begin to change her beliefs to support a more positive and productive view of herself.

We need to use these kinds of negative thoughts to bring

awareness into our lives, enabling us to explore why they are there, then to begin to let go of them and to move forward. I write more about this in Chapter Four.

The common denominator

If you think back on your life, you will realise that there is one common denominator in all the situations you have been in – and that is you. Only you have been in absolutely every experience in your life. Consequently you have something to do with each event happening. How you think and act in response to an event means that the outcome may be quite different in each case – but the one common element is your presence.

> I first realised this at about twenty one, when I was reflecting on my relationships with the boys I'd been out with, and realised that I was there with each one of them – I was the common denominator and therefore maybe I had something to do with how each relationship evolved (or not!). This was a major breakthrough for me in my willingness to be responsible for myself in my life.

Anything is possible

It is important to remain open to all possibilities – there are many, many ideas that we do not, as yet, know about. Change brings all kinds of things that we simply wouldn't have thought possible before. History is full of examples like this – the world being imagined as flat, or the idea of a man on the moon being preposterous.

In respect of using our thoughts to change our circumstances, it is important to realise that if we state 'I welcome changes into my life', then we must be prepared for changes to happen. If we state 'I attract plenty of money' then we must be prepared for plenty of money to come our way – and although that may seem like a dream come true, it may also bring unexpected responsibilities. There are always consequences from all our thoughts, just as there are always consequences from our actions. It makes sense, therefore, to become as aware as possible of what we are thinking, so that we can choose to think thoughts and images that will support us rather than ones that will hinder us.

Chapter Two

HOW DO POSITIVE AFFIRMATIONS ACTUALLY WORK?

Your internal boxes and filing system

Imagine a huge storage system composed of many boxes inside your mind. Each box is full of files covering different areas, such as money, pleasure, work, sex, love, health, self-image and so on. One of your boxes might be labelled 'Relationships', and inside there will be a whole series of positive and negative files about relationships. Some of the limiting, negative thoughts stored in those files might be 'Relationships never seem to work for me', 'There are no decent women/men out there', or 'Men/women always let me down'.

Another box might be labelled 'Health'. Inside, some of the negative thoughts filed away might be 'Anyone who gets ill must be really weak', or 'If flu is around, you can be sure I'll be the one to pick it up'.

Often, we have so many negative ideas about a subject that they overwhelm any positive ones we may have, and we become unable to think about that subject in any way other than negatively. Over the years, we have created hundreds of files to put in our boxes, each determined by our experience of life. So an initial experience of jealousy might be amplified by further experiences of jealousy, leading to a box labelled 'I am a jealous person', and including files such as 'I'm jealous of my sister' or 'Jealousy is a sign that I care'.

Familiarity

It is easier for us to take in an idea that is already familiar to us – if we already have a file made up about this idea in one of our boxes, it then becomes very easy to take in another associated idea and file it away. For instance, if we have a box labelled 'Intelligence', and in that box various files relating to the idea 'I'm unintelligent', then when we hear, see or feel anything that might be similar to this idea (like 'You're such an idiot!') it confirms the original idea, and the file begins to bulge even more with ideas associated with 'I'm unintelligent'. This all happens so automatically that we don't even realise we are doing it.

If your boxes are mainly full of negative ideas, then when you hear a positive idea about yourself, you won't know where to file it. When you use positive affirmations you will have to take some time to create a box to store all the new positive images and thoughts. As you can imagine, it takes more energy, effort and time to make up a new file for an idea you haven't heard before than it does simply to slot a familiar idea into a well-known negative file.

What are some of your negative boxes?

Many of us have more negative thoughts in our boxes than positive. In fact, some of us may be so unused to hearing or saying good things about ourselves that very few, if any, positively labelled boxes exist. To begin to explore your own filing system, notice your reactions to the following statements, and note your response in your journal. Do you have boxes labelled with these ideas or something similar? Do you agree with these ideas (and therefore have a box of this name), or do you disagree? If you do disagree, then what do you think about that statement? What boxes do you have in relation to these ideas?

BOX	EXAMPLE FILE TITLES
My country	This country is going to the dogs
Life in general	My life is a big mess 'Life just isn't fair'
Need for approval	I just can't get things right
Work	My work is pretty boring really I'll never get promotion
Intelligence	I'm not very intelligent Other people are cleverer than I am I could do better
Money	I'll never have enough money More money would really solve all my problems
Relationships	I'm not happy with my partner We're always arguing Women/men just don't like me enough
Self-esteem	I'm not much good, really I don't deserve anything good in my life

If you find in doing this exercise that you have identified some negative thoughts, then the process is already working. Set these ideas aside for a moment – they will be very useful when you come to Chapter Four and to the exercises on discovering your negative beliefs.

Where do our files and boxes come from?

Many of our negatively labelled boxes have been with us as long as we can remember, or longer. We have (subconsciously) made them up as a result of picking up the same critical idea about ourselves over and over again. In our families whatever happens or is said on a regular basis not only becomes familiar, it becomes what we think of as normal – usually, for instance, until we go to school and discover that not everyone has only one parent, or that we are the only one not allowed to have schoolfriends home. Indeed, many boxes are made as a result of our experiences at school! This very early conditioning gives us our basic ideas about life and the world around us, which we categorise into our various boxes and files. As adults we often go on to experience life in similar ways to that which we experienced as a child. It is what we know, and is, therefore, more familiar and less threatening than what we don't know. Our boxes, in which we sit surrounded by our familiar negative ideas, often seem more appealing simply *because* we know them so well; getting out of the box, or entertaining the idea of other boxes filled with different ideas, can feel very unsafe – consequently the idea of changing can often seem like just too much effort.

This is why the idea of change can be so threatening sometimes. Our lives are often predictable and we feel as if we know what is going to happen, even if we don't like it very much. The prospect of something new or unknown creates apprehension in us; however, it can also be extremely stimulating creatively, and even exciting!

> Right from when I was a young teenager, I noticed that the night before a new job I would begin to see all the good things in my old job. I would begin to wonder why on earth I had ever wanted to change – my old job and the old way of working seemed not to be so bad after all. I would wish I wasn't leaving, and was usually filled with apprehension about what it would be like and how I would fit in in the new workplace. However, as soon as I had arrived at the new job, my feelings would change – as soon as 'the unknown' became 'known', I felt OK, whether or not I enjoyed the job. After some time I realised that these feelings were an entirely normal response to change, and that they occurred at all times in my life where I was about to enter into an unknown situation. I began to recognise this anxiety as par for the course, and I became more able to accept the feelings as natural. The less I resisted feeling them, the less they bothered me, and the more I began to understand and feel comfortable with myself.

Our childhood patterns

Small children relate to the world as though they are the centre of it, and often may think that something unpleasant was their fault, even subconsciously. They don't have the capacity to conceptualise in the way that adults do. When we *are* adult we *do* have the conceptual capability to catch our thoughts, and to question ourselves and our behaviour. We can see and understand that our beliefs and negative thought patterns are often the result of ideas we picked up in childhood, and that they contribute to our negatively filled boxes staying the same. These ideas may have been necessary in childhood, but in adult life they often become a hindrance, literally getting in the way of us enjoying our lives fully as adults.

> Peter was a thirty-five-year-old man who came to see me because he was becoming dissatisfied with his life. He could not understand what was happening, and did not know what to do. He was a diligent worker at his office, generally staying in the background, avoiding office politics, and was known as a good, steady guy. He lived alone, dressed in a nondescript way, and had few friends. In his relationships with women, he bent over backwards to be 'nice' to them and to avoid disagreements, and consequently found himself unable to stand up for himself. However, he wanted a long-term happy relationship, and to feel happier at work.

Exploring Peter's background, I heard that as a child he had witnessed many arguments between his parents. He had very quickly learnt that in order not to be shouted at himself, it was best to keep as quiet as possible and out of the way. He treated his bedroom as a sanctuary, but was so worried about the arguing that he would sit at the top of

How do positive affirmations actually work?

the stairs to listen, so that he would find out if his parents were going to divorce or not (his biggest fear). As soon as he heard them come out of the living room, he would run back to bed to hide. He had tried his hardest to be a 'good boy', because he knew from experience that when he misbehaved, it would be an excuse for his parents to argue again.

Together we explored the fact that as a child Peter had done the best he could to protect himself in what he found a very threatening environment. However, this learnt behaviour as a child was now getting in the way of his enjoyment of life as an adult. He was still trying to protect himself from possible harm, just as he had done with his parents. This took the form of staying in the background at work, and of avoiding all possible disputes with partners. Peter realised that his beliefs in these areas had been formed as a result of his childhood experiences, and that by his behaviour now, he was, in turn, perpetuating them in adulthood. In other words, he was continuing to add to his negative boxes. Over time, Peter began to understand and accept why he was the way he was, and by using positive affirmations and other techniques he was able to make the changes he wanted in his life.

Getting out of a negative box

It is possible to get out of a box of negativity in which you might be sitting (even if your ideas seem deeply entrenched). You begin to affirm positively who you are and what you do. You change your negatively labelled boxes into positive ones; and then you get to sit in whatever box you wish, surrounded by your choice of positive thoughts. This is a process in itself, and will take time – Chapter Four will tell you how to start.

Chapter Three

CHALLENGES TO THINKING POSITIVELY

Worrying about what's in your box

Some of you might find yourselves thinking 'Oh dear I'm not sure I want to know what is in my box'. Please don't let this put you off exploring yourself in this way. Only the negative ideas *you are ready to look at* will jump out and be caught by you. The others will simply stay where they are, in your unconscious, until you are really ready.

Objections to positive statements

When you state something positive about yourself that does not have a box of its own inside you, you often bring to your conscious mind your objections to that phrase from an existing associated negative box. If you say to yourself 'I am a loving and lovable human being,' and you don't believe that, you are likely to have a response such as, 'No I'm not, don't be so ridiculous'. This tells you that you don't consider yourself loving or lovable. When we say something positive about a situation, if it conflicts with our internal thoughts then it's almost as if all the contents of that box come out one by one to fight against this new idea. They try to prove that we are wrong, and in fact they do such a good job that often when people first start this process their negative responses are so strong that they think the affirmations aren't working. But this is one of the main ways they *do* work. We say something positive, and this activates our (perhaps subconscious) negative ideas about this – they jump out of the box, we catch one of them, *and we get to see what was in the box in the first place* – we get to know ourselves better. Our negative thoughts become more conscious, and when a thought is conscious, it no longer has so much control over us, simply because we can choose to change it.

> I first noticed this myself when writing affirmations on a beach in Thailand, many years ago. I was writing 'I am a beautiful and capable woman'. All my responses were negative and I kept having to face the idea that I thought I was definitely incapable (having just been made redundant was confirming this idea), and I certainly wasn't beautiful, because if I was, then where was the wonderful man who was attracted to me? This was my thinking at the time. Some time later, having moved on from that affirmation to other ones, I came across the old notebook in which I'd been writing, and as I read 'I am a beautiful and capable woman' I realised that I now not only believed this idea, but somehow inside, I knew it. I had come to view my redundancy as a gift which had propelled me into new ways of living and thinking, and although I wasn't at that time in a loving and committed relationship, I had discovered many of the reasons why that was so. My life was changing.

Judging your negative thoughts

It is very easy to beat yourself up when you notice you are thinking gloomy thoughts or feeling low. Judging yourself often happens unnoticed at this point. Because 'thinking positively' has traditionally meant that you should always feel happy and contented, it is easy to get depressed when you find yourself thinking even more negatively than before, or if your situation seems to get much worse. This is why people often give up at this stage. But if you are willing to use positive thinking as a route to self-knowledge, then you can welcome any negative thoughts you have, because they provide you with so many insights about yourself. They become something to acknowledge, learn from and then let go of. Given this, you then have the choice to feel bad that you've said or thought something negative or to feel good about the fact that you've noticed it. You can even be grateful for the fact this thought exists and is showing itself to you! Give yourself a pat on the back for noticing that you had the thought – and then you will be able to begin the personal exploration of where that thought came from.

If things seem to be getting worse

When we say something positive to ourselves about our life, it literally causes internal friction as it rubs up against the negative idea in which we have always believed. It is this friction that causes us to feel uncomfortable while we are changing. Sometimes during changes, we find that we have all sorts of different feelings. One minute we feel great; our positive thinking seems to be working. But the next minute (sometimes literally!) we feel down in the dumps again, full of negativity and simply unable to see through the gloom to any spot of brightness at all. These uncomfortable feelings are a sign that the process is working.

You may find relatively few uncomfortable feelings. Sometimes you are so ready for change that your negative thoughts and files surrender without a struggle. However, if you do feel uncomfortable, know that it is a natural part of the process of change, and can be made much easier by finding support, either in the form of a workshop or course, individual counselling, a like-minded friend or a self-help support group.

Fear of change

It is often fear, or an associated feeling, that can get in the way of our desire to change. If you identify a fearful feeling, then take your time to explore why you are feeling like that. There is nothing to be gained from forging ahead, ignoring how you feel – you will only have to go back later to integrate whatever you missed on the way. Your fear is there for a reason – it may well be that change in the area you are considering is too much to cope with at that moment in your life (which doesn't mean that the next day it might no longer be too much to cope with!). If you are clear about this, then you can respond honourably to your feelings and accept that that is where you are right now; indeed, it is often the acceptance of a feeling that allows us to feel free of it, which in turn allows us to move forward.

On the other hand, don't let your fear stand in the way of your desires. Easier said than done – but again a lot can be gained if you are willing to look at why you are fearful.

Chapter Four

DISCOVERING NEGATIVE BELIEFS

The first step in beginning to change your negative beliefs is for you to know exactly what they are. You may already have identified some of these, in which case make a note of them now, before continuing. Being clear about your beliefs is the core element of how I use and teach positive thinking. When we are able to identify our negative beliefs, then we have the choice to change them or not. If we don't know who we are or what we think, what our values are, or what are our conditioned reactions to different situations in life, then we have missed the starting point. We need to discover what boxes we have inside ourselves, and what kinds of thoughts are in them.

We will start by investigating the negative beliefs we not only know we already hold, but also by exploring our past to see what negative ideas we may have picked up while we were growing up and which are still influencing us now as adults.

I use three main exercises to identify negative beliefs; I recommend that you work with what initially attracts you most (to get you started), and then come back to the others as you feel the need to explore further.

Exercise One   Negative family sayings

Exercise Two   Negative things you say now

Exercise Three   Storylines, dramas, and underlying themes

Exercise One: Negative family sayings

Family sayings, both positive and negative, are common phrases that you remember hearing over and over again, usually when you were a child, and which may still be said by your family today. As a child, they were normal to your household, and you may still be somehow subscribing to them as an adult. This exercise lets you examine exactly what they were, and what they meant, and how you may have taken them on board in your life.

An example of a negative family saying is, 'If you don't stop crying, I'll give you something to really cry about'. The message the child's subconscious mind might hear is that they are not allowed to feel their feelings; or that it is not OK to cry; or that they are going to be punished for feeling whatever they are feeling. They may also feel threatened. How exactly the child subconsciously interprets this family saying depends to a large extent on their family situation, but one clear message that does stand out is that the child's feelings are being denied. If a child receives this

Discovering negative beliefs

message over and over again, it is likely that they will integrate it to the point where, as an adult, they think that crying is not OK; or that they will be punished if they feel; or that their feelings will invoke somebody else's anger. It becomes a negative belief, which may then seriously affect their adult life.

> Melanie was a twenty-three-year-old young woman whose parents had recently divorced. She was feeling very distressed by this, striving to cope by throwing herself into her work. However, she was sleeping very badly, and this, along with work pressures, was taking its toll. Her doctor had suggested she see a counsellor. Melanie began to talk about her difficulty in expressing feelings in general, and specifically that she had been unable to cry since the divorce. In talking about her childhood, it appeared that neither Melanie nor her elder sister was encouraged to express their feelings; and indeed, tears were strongly frowned upon by both parents as being 'feeble', 'letting the side down', and 'a waste of time'. She was able to remember her father in particular criticising her for crying, often threatening her with the phrase, 'If you don't stop crying, I'll give you something to really cry about!'. As a child she had grown up thinking that she would be judged for crying – and she was still now acting this out in her life. Being with someone who encouraged her to cry was painful but also a huge relief, as Melanie began finally to grieve for the loss of her parents' marriage.

Some examples of family sayings are listed below – these are all actual examples given by participants in workshops. Make a note of the ones that belonged in your family, and add any others that come to mind.

As you do this exercise, pay attention to any feelings you might be having, and note them down too. It is often the case that the feelings we have now that are associated with particular thoughts are in fact feelings from our childhood experiences coming forward from the past into the present.

Warnings

People are not to be trusted
Be careful!
You'll be the death of me
Life is full of dangers

Advice

It's better to give than receive
Some things are better left unsaid
You should respect your parents

Feelings

Anger's not very attractive in a little girl
You're just jealous
I could kill you!
Big boys don't cry

Orders

Don't do as I do, do as I say

Work before play

Stop worrying...

Don't boss your elders

Put Downs

You're stupid/silly/no good/useless

Who's going to look at you!

Children should be seen and not heard

Could do better (in school)

You don't know what you're talking about

Why can't you be more like...

You're not wanted in this country

You may find that you don't actually remember any of these or other things being said specifically, rather you just picked up that this was the way things were in your family. For instance:

Don't do as I do, do as I say *(a confusing message for a child, who hears their parent saying one thing, but sees them doing exactly what they have been told not to do)*

Life is full of dangers *(if you had a parent who was agoraphobic, for example, or timid, or very scared for you, and always worrying about you)*

If ideas come to mind for you that you don't actually remember anybody saying, then jot them down too. Whether they were said or not, you probably picked them up from behaviour around you, body language, mixed messages and so on.

A message for parents

A word for parents reading this who may not be feeling too good because they've identified things they've either said in the past or are saying now to their children. We say these sorts of things because they are what we have learnt. How can we possibly say anything other than what we have learnt? Please be compassionate with yourself if you are feeling guilty – let the guilt go and tell yourself, 'I did the very best I could, given what I knew', or, 'I do the very best I can, given what I know'. If you recognise these sayings as what you say now, you can decide to notice exactly when you say them and choose to change them.

> Terry, who works from home, was looking after his eight-year-old son, Ben, one day during the holidays; they'd been out shopping and Ben was finishing an ice lolly. They were in the office when Terry turned to see Ben at the computer, his lolly dripping all over the keyboard. Out of Terry's mouth popped the words, 'Ben, I could kill you!'. Terry felt rather alarmed to hear himself say this, especially as it had been something he had heard often from his mother. He apologised to Ben, told him he didn't really mean it, and explained why he was angry. He also acknowledged to Ben that he could have asked him to stay out of the office while he was still licking his lolly. At this

point, Terry also chose to forgive himself as well – letting himself
know it was okay to make a mistake, and that he could learn from it.

We do the best we can, given what we know

This phrase is one of the most important you can use
when looking over your past and wishing it was different –
it is a phrase that spells forgiveness and letting go. It also
applies to those of us who feel angry, bitter, resentful and
blaming towards our own parents – you can say, 'They did
the best they could, given what they knew'. This may seem
extremely difficult to apply if a parent was abusive in any
way – the mind automatically thinks, 'But how could they
do a thing like that – it's unbelievable, disgusting!'. Thinking
that they did the best they could does not preclude you
feeling any of these things, nor does it condone their
behaviour – what it *does* do is allow you to move forward
in your life; it allows you to begin to halt any negative effect
your parents' behaviour had on you, and to move forward
into a more positive place.

By now you are well into your list of negative family sayings. You may find you have only noted down two or three
things; you may find you have a more lengthy list. There is
no right or wrong to achieve here – what you have put
down on your list is what is right for you. Now take some
time to examine whether these sayings have become a
negative statement that you still believe, which is still
affecting you in the present.

Exercise Two: Negative things you say now

Make a list of the critical thoughts you have about yourself now in relation to the different areas below, plus any others that come to mind. Also include any critical comments that others have made, or do make, about you, particularly anyone whom you regard as an authority figure. It doesn't matter whether or not you believe these ideas – put them down anyway so that you can take time to consider what effect, if any, they have (or have had) on your life.

Love and relationships (e.g. I'm not very successful in my love life)

Touch (e.g. I never get enough hugs; nobody ever wants to hug me)

Feelings (e.g. I hate these feelings I have; nobody would want to know me if I expressed how I really felt)

The body and health (and illness) (e.g. I hate my body; getting ill is feeble)

Sex (and your sexuality) (e.g. sex is dirty; I'm only wanted for sex)

Money (e.g. I never seem to have enough money; everyone else has money, but not me)

Work (and school) (e.g. I never get promoted; work's so boring)

Life itself (e.g. life is just so unfair; life is all doom and gloom)

God (e.g. God never gives me anything; I must please God otherwise something awful will happen)

For this exercise, set the kitchen timer for twenty minutes for the whole exercise; sit down with your paper and pen and keep focusing on the topics as best you can. Or you could get together with a group of friends; do the exercise as I suggest, and then discuss it together afterwards. Other people often can help us to identify our negative thoughts, and discussing them in itself may make you remember others you habitually think. Once again, there is no right or wrong to achieve. Keep this list so you can add to it if further ideas come to light later.

Exercise Three: Storylines, dramas, and underlying themes

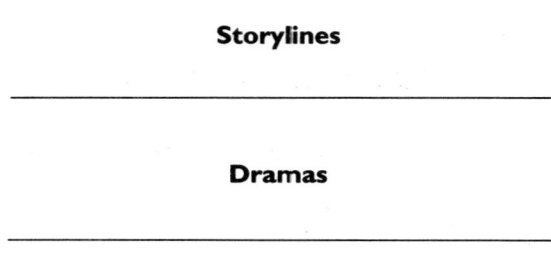

A *Storylines*

We can see life as a series of dramas, almost as if enacted on a stage. Some people have lives that seem to be more dramatically 'exciting'; others seem to have more placid lives. There is always a storyline to any drama that occurs, and although sometimes it is very obvious, we often need to look to discover what it is. For example, the person who is made redundant and then sets up a successful business with their redundancy payments; or someone who receives a lot of money and then loses it all gambling. These are what I call the storylines. In order clearly to state the storyline, we write down the facts of the situation in the third person and the present tense, keeping it to the point and short.

For example:

Megan's storyline

Megan has recently contracted breast cancer. She is reluctant to have a mastectomy but has been told that she will need the operation within the next three months. She wants to use this time to try to come terms with what has happened – she can't understand it, and is interested in finding out if her stressful lifestyle might have contributed in any way.

B *Dramas*

The drama is what is going on underneath the storyline, and although there may be some overlap with the storyline, it usually contains how we feel about a situation. One of the most fundamental questions that we can ask ourselves at this stage is: 'What is really going on here?'. By asking this question, you are searching for what is going on under the surface. 'What's really going on' is of course going to be different for each person, even if they are in similar situations, so this is a very personal question, and is answered by you, with whatever degree of self-knowledge you have. Focusing on the feelings is essential in helping you to identify what might really be going on. Again, it is written in the third person.

As this is a very powerful question, and involves us being willing to be as honest as we can be, we may find ourselves facing some scary feelings or facts; we may find ourselves unwilling to admit the extent of the situation we are in. This process is easier if we have some support; however, it is really important to take it gently, and work with what comes up for us, with as much kindness and compassion as we can give ourselves.

Megan's drama

What is really going on is that Megan is very tired; she has three young children; her husband is away often, and she feels very much alone. Her mother, who lives nearby, is house-bound at the moment, and Megan has taken on some of her care. Megan feels as if she is always there for everybody, but when it comes down to it, no-one is there for her. She feels like she takes care of the children and her mother and no-one takes care of her. She cannot imagine what will happen when she goes into hospital for the operation and she is not there to look after everyone, and is worried about it, but she feels desperate for all the demands everyone makes on her to stop.

As you can see, Megan's drama is full of feelings. They are:

- ◆ She feels very much alone.
- ◆ She feels as if she is always there for everybody, but no-one is there for her.
- ◆ She feels no-one takes care of her.
- ◆ She is worried about how her family will manage when she goes into hospital.
- ◆ She feels desperate because of all the demands everyone makes on her.

Putting these statements into the first person, Megan can identify some of her negative beliefs:

I feel very much alone
No-one is there for me
No-one takes care of me
Other people's demands overwhelm me
I'm worried how everyone will manage when I go into hospital

When Megan looked at her drama and list of beliefs she also realised another one – that it was not OK for her to have any needs of her own. In some way, for her, admitting she had needs was admitting she was a failure.

It is only when we assess the full situation, not just the storyline, that we give ourselves the opportunity to address our underlying tension and dissatisfaction and to ensure that our life circumstances can alter permanently. If we simply focus on the storyline, i.e. what is on the surface, certainly we may change the details, but the pattern is likely to stay the same. For example, if Megan gets someone else to look after her mother, some of the pressure will be off, but if she hasn't addressed her need to look after others, then she will sooner or later find herself back in the same position with others – feeling overwhelmed by their demands, and unable to do anything about it. She would become a victim of her circumstances once more.

C Themes

It is enormously valuable to discover any themes or patterns you may have in your life. Without realising it, you may have been repeating a detrimental pattern for years. This part of the exercise gives you an opportunity to identify any pattern that may exist, so that you can begin to let go of it, and any other negative beliefs you may have.

To identify a theme, you start off by looking back in your life to see if you can identify situations similar to your current one. Then look again to discover when you had similar feelings to the ones you are having now. Often it is the case that the circumstances will be very different, but the feelings will be similar. Read Megan's example below to get an idea of this.

Megan's theme

Megan began to look at other situations in her life where she had played the role of 'carer'. At college she had inadvertently adopted the role of taking care of others, and she was able to see that, in her own family where she was the eldest sister, she had always been responsible for her younger siblings, and spent a lot of her time looking after them. Indeed, her mother had relied on her to look after them. When looking at the feelings that were involved, she realised that as a child she had often felt resentful about having to look after her brothers and sisters; and similarly, when under stress herself at college, she would begin to tire of people coming to her for advice. The same feelings had been occurring lately. Realising all this, she understood that her breast cancer was stopping her short and forcing her to examine the cause of stress in her life. She resolved to become less of a 'carer' and to begin to think of herself more. She began to do this by having weekly counselling sessions, and thereby began a process of discovering some of her needs and allowing herself to have them met.

Discovering negative beliefs

At this point, Megan changed her negative beliefs into positive affirmations, which were designed to counteract the negative statements.

I feel very much alone	*became*	I have plenty of close friends
No-one is there for me	*became*	There is always someone there for me
I take care of the children and my mother and no-one takes care of me	*became*	More and more I feel taken care of myself
I need to take care of everyone around me	*became*	I no longer need to take care of everyone; I can let them take more care of themselves
Other people's demands overwhelm me	*became*	I can say no when I need to
I am worried about going into hospital	*became*	All is well, even when I'm not there
It's not okay for me to have needs	*became*	I acknowledge that I have needs and am willing to have them met

By working with these and other affirmations in ways described later, Megan began to fill her negative boxes with more positive messages. As she repeated these affirmations over and over, her negative responses to them gave her more clues as to why she was in this situation. In her reading about breast cancer, she realised that some links had been made between breast cancer and those women who tend to nurture others at the expense of themselves. (N. B. There are also other lifestyle factors that may contribute to breast cancer.) She began to understand that her intuition about exploring the part that her lifestyle could have played in her getting cancer was spot on; and that indeed her own lifestyle of caring for others without allowing herself to receive enough care was instrumental in the position in which she found herself. Megan decided to go ahead with the mastectomy, at the same time making radical changes in her way of living.

Before you proceed to identifying your own storylines, read through the following examples and underline the negative beliefs that these two people have. You will find my suggestions for their negative beliefs at the end of this chapter.

Example 1

Margaret's storyline
Margaret had identified that she always seemed to pick the 'wrong' men for her. She had had a series of dissatisfying, short-lived relationships, and couldn't understand why this was so, when she so badly wanted a long term, committed relationship.

Margaret's drama
Margaret began to explore what was really going on for her by acknowledging that the common denominator in all her relationships had been her, so maybe it was something in her that was 'wrong', as opposed to the men being 'wrong'. From this standpoint, Margaret began to look at

her own attitudes to commitment, and discovered that on the one hand it was something she really wanted, but on the other hand, she was rather alarmed by what commitment meant to her. What was really going on was that although she said she wanted a long-term relationship she also felt apprehensive about it.

What do you think Margaret's negative beliefs are?

Margaret's theme

When Margaret began to explore a possible theme, she began by analysing all the factors of each relationship on paper, and then looked for anything in common. What she discovered was that although all the relationships were very different, and with very different men, there was one major similarity amongst all the men – they simply were not available to have a long-term, committed relationship with one woman. They were either with a partner, or married, or only interested in travelling and so on. When she focused on her feelings, Margaret realised that she had invariably felt unwanted to some degree or another in all these relationships, which led to her feeling dissatisfied and always wanting more from these men. This was also similar to when she was younger and her father had only been around intermittently. When exploring how she felt about commitment, Margaret discovered that she was rather alarmed at the thought of committing herself to one person, in case they left her. From this point, Margaret began to understand that if she was uncertain about commitment then she was attracting and being attracted to men who were also not keen on it, and this was a perfect way to avoid facing up to her own fears. Her process continued over some time as she discovered why she was so scared and how exactly this was hampering her relationships. She began to explore her motives each time she found herself attracted to a man who was clearly not available. Some time later, she found herself attracted to a man who was also interested in a committed relationship, and they began living together successfully.

Example 2

Michael's storyline

Michael was unhappy in his work. He was in a high-powered position in a large company, but his working conditions had changed so much that he had too much to do of the kind of work that he most disliked. He was fed up.

Michael's drama

When Michael asked the question, 'What is really going on?' of himself, he admitted that he had changed in himself over the last three years. He was approaching forty, and was beginning to feel that time was passing him by. What had once satisfied him and been a challenge was no longer so. Coupled with less interesting work, he was feeling very disillusioned with life. However, when he thought of changing his job in any way, it made him feel very anxious, and he became full of reasons why it would be a silly idea, not least because he thought he would never find another one. He realised he needed to change, but was terrified of doing so.

What might Michael's negative beliefs be?

Michael's theme

When Michael explored other times in his life when he had felt anxious and unable to change his situation, he realised that this happened each time he was either in the middle of a practical change (such as when he had gone to boarding school), or when his circumstances had changed in

Discovering negative beliefs

some other way. In short, any change at all he found threatening. Exploring why this was the case, Michael began to see some links with a series of major changes in his childhood (the divorce of his parents, changing schools, his father's redundancy). His experience of change was that it happened to him and there was nothing he could do about it. So when he found himself feeling dissatisfied and actually wanting to change his circumstances, he also found himself experiencing some very scary feelings. This new understanding in itself went some way to alleviating Michael's fear, and over the period of the next year he began slowly to negotiate more satisfying work, and eventually found the courage to hand in his notice and work freelance for the company instead.

Identifying your own storylines, dramas and themes

Now it is time to specify your own storyline for whatever situation you are in.

Stage One: The Storyline

Focus on the facts; keep it short and to the point, and in the present tense.

Stage Two: The Drama

Focus on the feelings, still writing in the present tense. Ask yourself the question: **What is really going on?** and be as honest as you can with yourself. Be willing to stay with this question for some time, even days – you will know the answers to be true when you feel them 'clunk-click' inside.

From this, identify your negative beliefs and write them down in the first person, as in the example with Megan. At this stage, all you need do is underline your negative beliefs; making up affirmations to begin to counteract them comes after looking for a theme – the third stage.

Stage Three: Looking for a theme

Now is the time to explore whether or not you have a theme or pattern in your life around these feelings and thoughts. There is not always a theme, but it is certainly worth looking for one. Start by looking for events in your past that were similar to the one you have just described. You may not identify any – in which case look for situations you were in where the thoughts and feelings were the same as those you have just described. Do this by simply listing on paper the different situations, and then have another column for the thoughts, feelings and memories that you associated with these situations. You may end up with a long list, and that's fine!

Having listed the differences, look for the similarities in these situations. This will lead you to common themes. You may find further negative beliefs arise which you can add to your list.

Having identified your negative beliefs, keep your notes on this so that you can add to them as you discover more, and also so that you can see those you actively don't believe anymore. It can be very encouraging to see, on paper, any changes you have made.

Suggestions for Margaret's negative beliefs:

I always pick the wrong man; there's something in me that's not right; I am alarmed by the idea of commitment.

Suggestions for Michael's negative beliefs:

I'm unhappy at work; I'm fed up; time is passing me by; I'm disillusioned with life; I'm scared of changing my job.

Chapter Five

USING AFFIRMATIONS

Having identified negative beliefs using the methods in the previous chapter, you can now begin the process of changing them by using positive affirmations. When you begin doing this, you will find that you experience all sorts of changes, both within and without, if for no other reason than that you are reflecting on your beliefs and attitudes. I often use the following metaphor to describe the process of using affirmations:

Imagine a stone being thrown into a pond. It sinks to the bottom, stirring up debris and mud on the way. The water may become murky and difficult to see through. Various bits and pieces may float to the surface, only to sink to the bottom again when the water stills.

Now imagine that that stone is like your affirmations, being thrown into the pond of your unconscious. They cause a disturbance; you may feel as though you can't see very clearly for some time; and things float to the surface, that is, to your conscious mind. These things are going to be new ways of thinking, memories, different feelings, or a new perspective on life. Maybe activities that you've always enjoyed doing will be seen in a different light, or experienced in a new way. When these things come to the surface, you have the opportunity of examining them and exploring why they were in your pond. The act of examining them means they become conscious, and can no longer sink down into the pond again. If you choose not to examine something that comes to the surface, then it will just sink down, and come up again at a later date. The ripples that occur as you throw in the affirmation can be seen as the effect on people around you – a kind of 'knock on' energy.

Adding to your positive boxes and files

Using affirmations to add to the number of positive files and boxes you already have inside yourself means that whenever you listen to affirmative messages on a tape, those in the lyrics of a song, or read them in a book, this is what's happening. You might even be doing something else while you are listening – driving, housework, or travelling to work. When you use positive affirmations in this way, your focus is simply on letting the ideas flow into and wash over you as much as you can, almost as if you were lying in the shallows of the warm tropical sea, with the gentle waves lapping at your sides. The intention is not particularly to notice your negative reactions to the affirmations (although this may well happen); it is to help your brain to prefer hearing positive statements rather than negative ones. If you want to make affirmations to which you are listening more personal to you, then use my *Making Changes* tape, where there is space for you to participate by repeating the affirmation to yourself. Using affirmations in this way allows you to incorporate affirmations into your daily life with very little disruption.

As you focus on listening to or reading affirmations, begin to notice how many negative messages are around in the world today – for instance, in the newspapers. Try stopping reading your newspaper or watching the news on TV and see how you feel. If you want to be kept in touch with current affairs, listen to the news bulletins on a radio, where the input of negativity is relatively short.

When you listen to music, really pay attention to the lyrics. You might be surprised at the content – love songs, in particular, are often about how unsuccessful relationships are, and how sad and depressing life is. Ask yourself if you want to be bombarding your mind with these kinds of ideas anymore.

As you change, you might find that some films or television programmes that you previously loved begin to get on your nerves, simply because of the negative messages. In short, you will begin to view life differently.

Positive affirmations can also be used to remind yourself that all is well and disaster is not just around the corner. Often, when we are in the middle of a drama or crisis, we automatically think the worst; or we can only see the negative side of things. The more you work with positive thinking to help you become aware of your thoughts and feelings, the easier it will be for you to remind yourself of another perspective in your life; to remind yourself that there is another way to see your situation.

Affirming life itself

I have been helped considerably in my journey through life by my beliefs and personal 'knowledge' of what some people would call 'God'. I believe that there is 'something' much greater than we are, as human beings, and that we can develop our relationship with this so that it becomes a source of strength and support for us. I don't think it matters what it is called, whether it is the Life Force, God, the Universe, Love, your Higher Power or Higher Self, Divine Spirit – whatever. The important thing is that there is a friendship, a well of love and strength that we can draw from, and that it is already within us and surrounding us, if we are only able to open our eyes to it. It is usually the times that we forget this when we feel at our lowest, lost in the dark and completely alone in the world. So that we don't forget it, we can affirm the presence of this friendship.

Before you read further about how to create your own affirmations, you might like to remind yourself of the principles outlined in Chapter One.

Guidelines to creating affirmations

There are several guidelines to creating affirmations that I have put together over the years. If you follow these, you will always be using the best possible ways to support yourself.

1 Keep them positive! Rather than stating what you don't want ('I don't want to be unappreciated at work any

Using affirmations

longer'), state what you do ('I am appreciated for the work that I do'). You may well have a negative reaction to this statement, but if you didn't have negative thoughts and feelings at this stage, you wouldn't be needing to make a positive affirmation about it!

2 **Make sure it's in the present tense.** If it is in the future tense then you will be stating that it will be true tomorrow, never today, now. An example of this is saying 'I will be kind to myself'. The temptation here is to think 'Yes I will – after I've just done this', or 'Yes I will – starting tomorrow morning'. An affirmation is something we state as if it were true *now*, even though we may not believe it or have any experience of it in our lives at this time.

3 **Work with words that are right for you.** By all means use affirmations that I or others suggest, but if some of the words are not right for you, then replace them with ones that are. Otherwise you are going to be doing someone else's affirmation, and while that will still work, it will be less powerful for you. As you practise, you will discover which affirmations feel right – you will have a sense of 'yes!' – even if you don't believe it. Participants in workshops often experience this as a 'clunk-click' inside, or sometimes a feeling of dread combined with excitement.

4 **Say them with feeling.** If you are saying affirmations out loud, do it with feeling! Even if you feel silly, or

don't believe the affirmation, say it *as if* you do. You will find you feel much better than if you simply mutter them, or say them doubtfully.

5 Keep them shorter rather than longer. This will make them easier to remember, and reduce the risk of you drifting and simply saying it to yourself parrot fashion, without feeling.

6 Make sure you are counteracting a negative belief. If you are changing a specific negative belief you know you have, be as clear as you can be about what that belief is, and then use words to counteract that belief. For example, if you know you would like to be more confident, first of all do some homework (see previous chapter). Discover exactly when and where you would like to feel confident, and identify specific negative beliefs about your self-confidence. They might be something like, 'I am so shy I can't even say hallo to strangers', or maybe, 'I feel confident about my work, but when it comes to teaching others I'm just hopeless – all my confidence goes out the window'. Having identified these, you can then make up a positive thought specifically to counteract these beliefs. These might be, 'I find it easier and easier to say hallo to people I don't know', and, 'I am a confident teacher'.

7 Use an affirmation that is easy to imagine – or to which you can easily attach an image. For example, 'I now attract a loving and supportive relationship'. When

I first used this, I imagined myself walking along a beach, arm in arm with a lovely man who loved me. I was feeling loved and cherished – and we looked great together! If you find it difficult to imagine yourself as if your affirmation were true, then pick an image you really like, such as a sunflower, or a rose, or a stream, and attach your positive statement to that. Then every time you see this symbol, you will be reminded of your affirmation. This will happen even if you are not consciously aware of it.

8 **Make it an 'alive' message, rather than a wish.** You will be able to sense when an affirmation has a feeling of movement and vitality about it, and when not. For example, 'I am rich' is a positive thought which follows all the guidelines here. It is in the present tense, short, positive, and probably counteracts a specific negative belief. It is, however, what I would call 'dead'. Compare it with 'Riches of all kinds continuously flow into my life' and you will see the difference.

Compiling an affirmation step-by-step

I have found that when beginning to counteract a negative belief, it is often easier to follow a relatively gentle procedure of affirmative statements, rather than jumping in the deep end immediately. You can start at any step, depending on what feels right. If this appeals to you, begin your affirmations using the following sequence:

Step One: I am willing to release the need...

Step Two: I release the need...

Step Three: I am willing to...

Step Four: I deserve to...

Step Five: I allow myself to...

Step Six: I now...

Using Margaret's example from earlier, having identified some of her negative beliefs, she began by using the affirmation, 'I am willing to release the need to feel scared of commitment'. After practising this for a few days, she realised she *was* willing to release this need, and moved on to 'I release the need to feel scared of commitment'. After some time, Margaret felt ready to move on again, and used the affirmation, 'I am willing to be in a committed relationship with a loving man'. This brought up quite a lot of her fears, which she explored, albeit sometimes with some uncomfortable feelings. One of her biggest fears was that being committed would make her very vulnerable to being hurt. However, after using this positive thought for some time, she once more felt ready for the next step, and began to use, 'I deserve a loving, supportive and committed relationship with a man'. Her negative responses to this affirmation were very much to do with her low sense of self-esteem, so at the same time she began saying, 'I am a worthy, lovable woman'. Eventually she felt more comfortable with this idea and moved on to 'I allow myself to attract a loving, supportive and committed relationship with a man'. At this stage she also made a list of all the qualities she considered her ideal relationship to have, so that she could be clear in her own mind, which is immensely helpful when coming to recognise whether a particular relationship is right for you or not. Her final affirmation was, 'I now attract a loving, supportive and committed relationship'.

Practising counteracting negative statements with positive affirmations

Here are some examples of negative beliefs and my suggestions for positive affirmations to counteract them, following the step-by-step sequence. Next to them is a space for you to make up your own affirmations to counteract the belief. You can do this exercise for practice and confidence before you begin on your own negative beliefs, checking them against the guidelines.

Negative belief
No-one appreciates me at work

Example affirmations:

- I am willing to release the need to feel unappreciated at work

- I release the need to feel unappreciated at work

- I am willing to experience appreciation at work

- I deserve appreciation at work

- I allow myself to be appreciated at work

- More and more, all that I do now at work is appreciated

Your own affirmations:

Negative belief:
I keep on having abusive relationships

Example affirmations:

◆ I release the need to be abused in my relationships

◆ I am willing to have only loving and supportive relationships in my life

◆ I deserve a loving and supportive relationship

◆ I allow myself to enjoy a loving and supportive relationship

◆ I now attract a loving and supportive relationship

Your own affirmations:

Negative belief:
I can't ask for what I want

Example Affirmations:

◆ I am willing to know what I want, and then ask for it

◆ I deserve to have what I want

◆ I find it easier and easier to know what I want, and then to ask for it

◆ It is now easy for me to recognise what I want, and then allow myself to have it.

Your own affirmations:

Negative belief:
I just can't feel angry

Example affirmations:

◆ I am willing to experience the feeling of anger

◆ I allow myself to feel angry when necessary

◆ It is easier and easier for me to feel my angry feelings

◆ I now am able to feel angry when I choose

Your own affirmations:

Practising your affirmations in this way is much easier if you have some support to help you. This is why joining a group or workshop works so well; if you are unable to do this, you might like to consider taking my correspondence course. For details of workshops and courses, see Appendix A.

Changing your negative thoughts and beliefs into positive ones

Now you are ready to turn back to your own list of negative beliefs and begin to counteract them by making up your own positive affirmations. If you want more practice, go back to the examples of Margaret and Michael and create affirmations for their negative beliefs, before starting on the next chapter.

Chapter Six

Practising Your Affirmations

Writing them down

One of the major ways I have used affirmations in my life and in all my workshops is by writing them down with my responses. This is a very powerful way to explore who you are, because you can't escape from it when it's written down in black and white. For each positive affirmation you write, you will find you have a response of some kind, either neutral, positive or negative. These responses will give you insights into what your beliefs and values are on the subject you are examining.

To start this, take a sheet of paper lengthwise and divide it into two with a line down the middle. Head the left hand column 'Affirmation' and the right hand column 'Response'. Now write your affirmation in the left hand column, and then your response to it on the right. Your response can be anything at all – it may be positive or negative; it may be 'don't know', or 'NO!'; you may even feel as though you have no response, or that your mind is wandering. If this is the case, then write that down, ie 'My mind is wandering'. You may simply notice a feeling or sensation in your body.

Having written your affirmation and response to it once,

go back to the left hand column and write your affirmation (the same one) again, and again write your response, which may be the same as before or different. It may also be how you are feeling (e.g. I'm fed up doing this affirmation!) – and in fact it is very important to notice how you are feeling as you do this process. Note down what you notice. Continue in this way until you have written your affirmation with a response a minimum of ten times. I recommend you do this process at least twice a day, say, in the morning and in the evening, so that it becomes part of your daily routine. Each time you do it, look back at what your responses were. What do they tell you about yourself in relation to your affirmation?

The following is an example from one of my workshops:

Beth had identified a series of negative beliefs associated with her extremely busy life, which left her exhausted and feeling empty. She narrowed this down to a central belief 'I just can't relax at all; I must keep going'. She composed a positive thought to counteract this which was, 'It is easier and easier for me to slow down and relax'. When writing this in the workshop, she came up with the following responses:

Affirmation

It is easier and easier for me to slow down and relax

It is easier and easier for me to slow down and relax

It is easier and easier for me to slow down and relax

It is easier and easier for me to slow down and relax

It is easier and easier for me to slow down and relax

It is easier and easier for me to slow down and relax

It is easier and easier for me to slow down and relax

It is easier and easier for me to slow down and relax

It is easier and easier for me to slow down and relax

Response

No it isn't

Don't be silly

Yes, but if I did that then nothing would ever get done

I can't

No, I just can't

I've got too much to do

Oh help

I'm scared of slowing down

Oh help, I'm scared

Looking back over these, Beth was interested to see that she clearly believed nothing would get done unless *she* did it. She was also surprised to observe that she was scared of slowing down. When she asked herself why this might be so, she realised she was terrified of what might happen while she was relaxing – of what she might feel. She decided to approach relaxation slowly and steadily, and came up with ideas of how she could slow down without feeling too scared, for example, by walking more slowly, or driving less hurriedly – not necessarily major steps, but a definite start.

The benefits of writing down your affirmations are:

- ◆ you can see what your negative reactions are very clearly on paper, which gives you the opportunity to explore them;

- ◆ it is very encouraging to see that, over time, your responses change from negative to more positive;

- ◆ the discipline of writing them down specifically interrupts the tyranny your negative thinking can have over you.

We don't need to limit ourselves only to writing affirmations – the more ways we can begin to challenge our habitual thought patterns the better. In fact, best results come when we incorporate many different ways of practising affirmations, choosing the ones that work best for us so that we enjoy the process and have plenty of variety. Below are some of the other techniques that I have used to bring affirmations into my life.

Making affirmative notices to put around your house

With this way of using affirmations, your aim is to be able to put up cards and drawings with your affirmation on wherever you want. This can be achieved step by step, ini-

Practising your affirmations

tially by putting them up where you feel safe, and then as you become more confident, you can put them up in other places.

> I had the positive saying 'I am a beautiful and capable woman' on my bedside table. My parents were coming to stay, and were going to be sleeping in our room. I had intended to put the affirmation away, but forgot. When my father came down from taking up their overnight bag, he walked up to me, gave me a big hug and said, 'You *are* a beautiful and capable woman!'. I felt wonderful – and very glad that I had left my affirmation out!

So you never know what might happen. Be brave – take a risk! Your positive thought can quite easily become a point of learning for other people too, maybe in a way that you wouldn't expect.

However, there is no point having an affirmation up that is going to make you feel bad because of the fear of others' reactions. This was the case with Sally, who had had an emotional time during an evening course I was leading. Initially she had found it impossible even to write down her positive thought. I encouraged her to take as much time as she needed, and over the next few weeks she progressed from writing it down and hiding it, to putting it in her sock drawer, where she saw it just once a day. Eventually she was able to have it out on her dressing table. She felt very good about her progress and had been able to see her confidence growing at the same time.

So use your instincts and common sense. Don't be hard

on yourself – it really defeats the object if you begin to feel bad about yourself because you don't want to put your affirmation up! Instead, put it in your diary, or a special drawer somewhere, or your purse or wallet. Treat yourself with kindness and compassion and don't try to forge ahead too quickly.

There are several ways of making yourself affirmative notices. Firstly, you can write your affirmation onto small pieces of card. Put them in places where you are likely to see them often, maybe around your kitchen sink, on the fridge door, above the television, on the bathroom mirror, in your car, or on your computer. You will find yourself noticing your affirmation when you're not consciously thinking about it, and even subconsciously it will lodge in your mind and begin its process of helping you to change for the better your attitudes and beliefs. You might also have a blackboard on which you can easily write and change your affirmations.

You can also draw your affirmation, or make a collage (see Appendix D). Take pleasure in its creativity as well as in the affirmation. The benefits of using affirmations in this way are:

◆ you will be reminded of your affirmations at all sorts of odd moments;

◆ you can easily change the cards when you want to change your affirmation;

◆ you allow healing creative expression at the same time as changing your mental thought pattern;

◆ you are using both the left and right hand sides of the brain, which makes a positive thought more powerful.

Using a mirror

Many people find it very difficult to look in the mirror and say nice things about themselves. We are simply not used to it – in fact, more often than not, when we look in a mirror we will be criticising ourselves. What happens when you go into the bathroom first thing in the morning, or look in the hall mirror before you go out? Notice what you are thinking about yourself – I can guarantee you will be judging yourself in some way, and probably negatively (especially in the morning!).

With mirror work, I suggest that you start in an entirely different way. Your intention is to look at yourself through your eyes. You might find this difficult to do at first, you may become shy or embarrassed, but take it step by step, and it will get easier.

I suggest you begin mirror work by standing in front of a mirror, when no-one else is around, and say your own personal affirmation, or 'I approve of myself', or 'I'm OK'. Notice your reactions – your feelings, and the thoughts you have in response. Allocate yourself one minute initially, and say the positive thought over and over again to yourself in your mirror. Be aware of how you are saying it and what you are feeling and thinking. Build this up to five minutes at a time, and when you feel more comfortable with the notion of mirror work itself, try sitting down in front of a large mirror and talking to yourself positively.

Particularly if your affirmation is about your body or health, then do take some time to stand without clothes on in front of a full-length mirror and say your affirmations. Again, notice what you think and feel – this is vital information for you in your journey of self-discovery. Your feeling and thinking responses and reactions are what are getting in the way of your health and happiness – if you become aware of them then you can begin to let them go.

> When I first started doing mirror work on my own I was living in a bamboo hut on the edge of a holiday centre in Greece. No-one was around; no-one could see or hear me – but I still looked over my shoulder before whispering, 'I love and approve of you'. I can remember feeling a bit daft! After some days I became much more confident, and this eventually led me to be able to look at myself in a full-length mirror more objectively and lovingly than I had ever done before. I began to view and treat myself with love, and accordingly, so did others.

The benefits of mirror work are:

◆ It is particularly good for those with physical challenges;

◆ You come face to face with yourself, literally, just as you come face to face with your thoughts on paper;

◆ You begin to counteract some of the negative messages you received face to face from others when you were small.

The power of imagery

To enhance the power of positive thoughts, actively use

Practising your affirmations

your imagination when thinking them. To do this, have your affirmation clear in your mind. Take a few moments to relax by firstly noticing your breath and bringing your attention to inside your body. As you breathe, you can begin to relax. Then ask your subconscious mind for an image to represent your affirmation. Pay great attention at this point, because the first thing that comes to mind, even if you think it is ridiculous, is likely to be the most powerful for you. It is amazing how accurate and appropriate this can be. Your image may be of yourself when your affirmation is true; or it may be something seemingly unconnected. If you have difficulty in finding an image then consciously choose something that you would like to represent your affirmation.

When you have an image, take some minutes to really explore it. Some of you will 'see' this image, others will 'hear', 'sense' or 'feel' it more; whatever comes for you is perfect for you, and it will become easier with practice. Explore all aspects of this image – look at it from all angles, so that you become very familiar with it. The more you do this the more you are inviting the creative, intuitive side of your brain to connect with the logical side which is thinking your affirmation. The benefits of imagery are:

◆ when we use both sides of the brain in this way it results in a more powerful message being given to our subconscious;

◆ creative daydreaming in this way is a relaxation.

Making your own tape

These days it is relatively easy to record your own voice, so you can use this to your benefit and record yourself saying positive messages. Start by making yourself a script of all your favourite or most appropriate affirmations, maybe about a particular area of your life. Think about it as if you were telling these lovely things to someone else for whom you really care. Use the first and the third person, for example, 'I find it easier and easier to value myself', and 'You (your name), find it easier and easier to value yourself', so that you are really reinforcing the message. You may also find that your affirmations make up a loving message for yourself (which you may even choose to sing!), such as: 'I am a beautiful and loving person. I live my life in the best way that I can, and learn continuously about who and what I am. I enjoy learning and exploring and I treat myself with kindness and compassion'. The benefits of making your own tape are:

◆ hearing your own voice telling yourself positive messages directly counteracts your own inner negative voice;

◆ the tape can be played while you are doing something else;

◆ each time you play it, you will focus on different aspects.

Practising your affirmations

Using your affirmation when you exercise

As you exercise your physical body, consciously say your affirmation over and over in time to the music in an exercise class, or while you are running or at the gym. You might associate different exercises with different positive thoughts, so that your mind automatically thinks of that particular thought as soon as you begin the exercise. If you love dancing, then use your affirmations in this too. Dance your positive thoughts – let your body move them for you. Begin to connect your mind and your body in this way – it can be really wonderful. The benefits of this are that you give yourself a mental workout at the same time as a physical one; and by incorporating your mind and your body, your affirmation becomes more powerful, just as when you are using your left and right brain.

Saying your affirmations with a partner

If you have a friend or partner who is also exploring themselves in this way, then you can support yourself actively by saying your affirmations to each other. There are two ways to do this:

1 Sit down facing each other, having decided who will be A and who B. B will tell A their affirmation, and A will repeat it back to B in the following way:

   A: ". . . . . . . (B's name), you are a beautiful, creative and intelligent woman".

   B: "Yes, thank you, I am!"

   Continue in this way for ten or fifteen times, saying the same affirmation, and then swop over, with B saying to A whatever A's affirmation is. This is an immensely loving way of supporting each other.

2 A says B's affirmation as before, but this time B says whatever her response is – the first thing that comes into her head – and A writes it down for her. Again, do this ten or fifteen times, and after the last time, B thanks A in whatever way feels appropriate.

The major benefit of these exercises are that you are likely to have a sense of loving support between you.

You may find plenty of other ways to practise your affirmations – be inventive! Whatever works for you is what is healthy and healing for you.

The three Ps

These are:

Practice

As in any new skill you learn, the more often you practise, the quicker you will see results. This is easy to see if you think of learning a musical instrument – one day you cannot make sense of the music, and some time later, after practising, you are able to produce a tune. With affirmations, it may be more difficult to see changes as they are often less quantifiable. So it is useful to reflect on your life every few weeks or so, making a list of all internal and external changes that you can think of.

Persistence

Do persist with practising your affirmations as much as you can. You may find yourself changing the emphasis in what you are saying relatively quickly, or even changing the affirmation after only a few days. This is fine – as you change, your affirmations will need to change. Persistence, however, does not mean that you cannot have a 'day off' from time to time. Whenever I have been writing affirmations, I make an agreement with myself that I will do them for, say, three days. Then at the end of three days I have a sense of achievement, and will make another agreement for maybe another three days. We need to make this process as easy as possible for ourselves, otherwise we are likely to just give up. I have had to find a way of practising that worked for me, so that I wasn't tempted to criticise myself for not doing my affirmations – which completely defeats the purpose!

Patience

This can be a real challenge to those of us who like to see instant results. I now think of the process of change as if it is a journey upstairs. On each step is something we need to know about ourselves to make our journey meaningful and fulfilling. This means that we have to be willing to tread on each step. Some of us, however, so badly want to get to the top step that we try and reach it in one or two leaps. Unfortunately, we miss out the steps in between – and often have to come back down so that we can go more slowly and find the message that each individual step has for us. Patience is our partner in this journey – if we rush on, we miss out on this valuable companionship.

Choosing to be great

All the time you are practising positive thinking in any of the ways described above, you are bombarding your subconscious mind with positive messages.

The more that we can inform our minds with these messages, the more fulfilment and satisfaction we will attract in our lives. It is too easy these days to follow the path of doom and destruction. It is a far greater challenge to choose to maximise our potential. As Marianne Williamson wrote in *A Return to Love: Reflections on the principles of A Course in Miracles,* (Harper Collins, 1992), and Nelson Mandela said in his inaugural speech:

> 'Our deepest fear is not that we are inadequate. Our deepest fear is that we are powerful beyond measure. It is our light, not our darkness, that most frightens us. We ask ourselves, Who am I to be brilliant, gorgeous, talented, fabulous? Actually, who are you not to be? You are a child of God. Your playing small doesn't serve the world. There's nothing enlightened about shrinking so that other people won't feel insecure around you. We are all meant to shine, as children do. And as we let our own light shine, we unconsciously give other people permission to do the same. As we are liberated from our own fear, our presence automatically liberates others.'

Chapter Seven

WHAT YOU FEEL, YOU CAN HEAL

Our feelings have a very strong relationship to our thoughts and behaviour. Take, for instance, the person who suffers a lot of rejection in their lives (the feeling), and then decides that they will never allow themselves to be rejected again (the thought), and so they avoid situations where this might be a possibility (the behaviour). The inter-relatedness of feeling, thought and behaviour means that when we want to make changes in our lives, we will be more successful if we are willing not only to consider our thought patterns, but also our associated feelings. In this chapter, I will be encouraging you to become more and more familiar with the huge variety of feelings available to you as human beings, so that you can use the information you receive to support you with your affirmations.

Getting to know your feelings

To begin the process of familiarising yourself with your feelings, bear in mind that conscious or subconscious feelings, even if they are not expressed, don't just go away; they continue to inhabit our bodies and express themselves in other ways, maybe through depression, over-excitement, or even as a physical disease. Over the last decade, psychoneuroimmunology, a field of science dealing with the connection between the mind and the body, has focused on showing that our emotions affect the chemical balances in our bodies, particularly our immune system.

Thus becoming 'friends' with our feelings, as well as our thoughts, is more than just a way of supporting ourselves in times of change – it is a positive and healthy action we can take to help keep ourselves in the best of physical health at all times.

Because we're usually approving in our society of the expression of so-called 'positive' feelings (such as joy, laughter, happiness and so on), it's often 'negative' feelings that are more difficult to acknowledge, let alone express. In fact, we are often so disapproving of feeling angry, crying or being frightened that we may do our very best to hide, suppress or deny that we have these feelings at all. Instead, we build up a screen behind which we can hide how we are truly feeling. It is this kind of falsity that contributes not only to disease, but also to such things as feelings of alienation from society, acute loneliness, inability to relate genuinely to others and depression, to name a few. Nevertheless, this can be changed. By gently becoming familiar with the range of feelings available to us, and by finding a way to express these appropriately (if we need to), we can begin to take the first small steps out from behind our screens and start to relate to others and the situations we find ourselves in from a more genuine and

What you feel, you can heal

healthy perspective.

If you choose to explore some of these feelings, the first thing to do is to know what the feeling means to you. This next exercise can be applied to any feeling you wish to explore; here we will address anger, sadness, fear, apathy and happiness.

Anger

How do you feel if you are angry? If you're not sure, look at the example on the following page.

You can see that by writing the feeling in the middle of the paper and then writing the words you associate with that feeling, you end up with your own personal understanding of what anger means to you. Do your own 'cluster' now, and make sure you include physical symptoms of anger as well as addressing the milder forms. If you find it difficult to think of any associated words, the list in Appendix B will help you.

Next time you notice any angry feeling, pay attention to how it expresses itself in your body – perhaps through feeling hot, a desire to shake someone, or stamp your feet, or an indignant tone of voice. Sometimes, especially if you tend towards addictive behaviour, you might find yourself eating, drinking, spending, or overworking to excess, as a way of displacing your feelings. If this is the case, when you realise you are being excessive in this way, think back to what sparked it off.

'Hidden' anger may also make its presence felt through

What you feel, you can heal

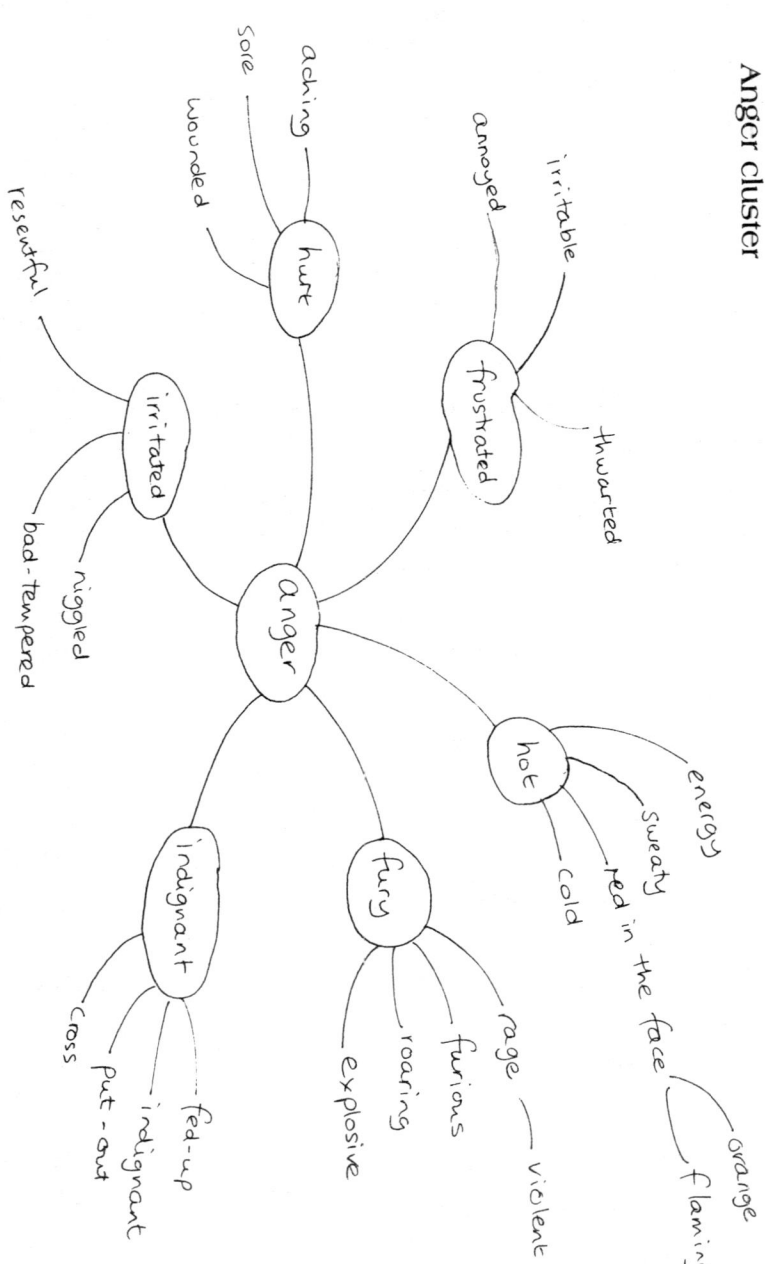

Anger cluster

sharp comments, jokes that aren't funny but rather cruel, digs at other people, coldness, or even sadness and withdrawal. You may also have heard of the theory that depression is anger turned inwards – while this may not always be the case, if you feel depressed, it is certainly worth exploring whether or not you also feel, or have felt, angry.

The more you are able to acknowledge and accept your feelings, the less they will interfere in your life in other ways. So the first step is to try to admit to yourself what you genuinely feel (this is where the cluster exercise helps). The next step is being able to express yourself in a more constructive manner, which, if you're angry, doesn't necessarily mean screaming and shouting at the person you're angry with – that might happen but it often isn't a successful way to resolve conflict. However, it *does* mean being able to express your feelings in a creative and appropriate way in order to be able to move forward from the situation feeling healthier and more in tune with yourself. For example, when angry, just saying 'I feel angry' in a loud tone of voice, several times, can begin to make you feel better. Other productive ways of expression could be through exercise or sports; yelling to a background of loud music; screaming into a pillow – any way in fact that enables you to let the feelings out, rather than keep them inside your body. Having let out this emotion, you may find the expression of feeling enough in itself to enable you to move forward; or if you are angry with a particular person, you may find it easier to communicate with them (they may also find it easier to hear what you are saying). Affirmations you could use to help you in this process might be: 'I am now in charge of my angry feelings'; 'I am willing to let myself feel angry'; or 'I express anger in appropriate ways when I choose'.

> Valerie was a woman in her mid-forties who gave an impression of gentleness and warmth. Married, and with two student children, she was concerned because she felt unable to stop spending money. This was causing difficulties in her marriage, as her husband could not understand why she couldn't limit herself to their budget. When she took the time to explore what had been happening just before each spending spree, it became clear to Valerie that there was a similar pattern to these occasions, resulting in her feeling put down in some way. Valerie was reluctant to say that she had felt angry, but upon exploring other words associated with anger, she realised that her main feeling had been irritation. At this point, she began to explore her thoughts and ideas about anger, and her family's attitude to it, which had been to ignore it completely. In fact, as a child, Valerie could remember thinking there was no point in getting angry, as it didn't make any difference. Over some time, Valerie was able not only to recognise her feelings but to accept them also. From this point, she moved forward to understanding that her overspending had been a way of trying to ignore her feelings of anger and irritation, which felt forbidden and uncomfortable to her. She began to admit to herself when she felt irritated, and then began practising expressing her irritation in words. As she did this, her need to overspend receded; the tension between her husband and herself became less; and she began to value herself more highly.

What you feel, you can heal

Often, it is easier to express angry feelings rather than the hurt that may be underlying them. This doesn't mean that the anger is unjustified or inappropriate – but if the hurt is not acknowledged, then the anger may persist for a longer time than is healthy. For instance, feelings of revenge are often a way to cover up how hurt or betrayed we feel. If we act on these revengeful feelings, the hurt doesn't necessarily go away – nothing will do that unless we are willing to acknowledge the extent of the hurt first. So, as well as expressing anger, any underlying feelings also need to be acknowledged.

Sadness

The same ideas apply to sadness. The more we are able to encompass this emotion as just one part of our lives, the less it will dominate overall. Doing the cluster exercise can help you understand sadness, but initially you need to become aware of what makes you sad (sad films can be excellent for this!) and how your body feels when it is sad – maybe a lump in your throat, a pricking behind your eyes, or a feeling of heaviness. Whenever you feel these sensations, rather than trying to make them go away, let them be there. Sadness is just as valid a feeling as any other, and has it's rightful place in our lives. Our bodies were created with tear ducts, and it can be immensely healing to use them!

If you find it relatively easy to cry, you may have noticed that the release of tears often seems to bring an easing of your emotions. You may then have been able to see your situation from a different perspective; often people describe the feeling after crying as 'cleansed', 'relieved', or simply just 'feeling better', enabling them to see things differently. This is because when we allow ourselves to feel what is there, rather than trying to suppress it, we make space for something else – the blockage created by the suppressed feeling disappears.

Becoming familiar with the quality of your tears can be very helpful – we may know about 'tears of joy' or 'tears of frustration' – but when you get to know your tears really well, you will find that sometimes you are crying ancient tears as if from when you were a toddler, or tears from a particular time in adolescence. Releasing these tears then lets you move on more effectively and completely into maturity and adulthood. Giving yourself permission to cry when you feel like it is one of the most nourishing things you can do for yourself. Other affirmations to help you with this might be 'I allow myself to cry', or 'I choose to express my sad feelings when I wish'. Sometimes people feel out of control of their tears, as if they are crying too much, too often, and I address this later on in this chapter.

Fear

Fear is another so-called 'negative' feeling, but it is also a life-saver in dangerous situations, causing adrenaline to pump through our bodies and enabling us to move from danger quickly. However, if it takes over our life, for instance, when it prevents us doing what we really want to do, it needs to be tamed. To do this, we need to be willing to experience fear, and then give it it's rightful place in our lives.

Fortunately, fear can also be exciting and productive; it keeps us on our toes, lets us know when something is not quite right, and can give us the necessary impetus to take action. Fear can be very close to excitement, and it is useful to be able to distinguish between the two to avoid inhibiting natural excitement. We can do this by becoming familiar with what fear feels like.

You will be able to identify ranges of this emotion much more easily if you appreciate the kinds of words you associate with fear – doing the cluster exercise will really help you with this. When we feel fearful, we can let ourselves feel it for an allotted period of time (say two minutes). We can begin to make friends with it so that then we don't have to fear the presence of fear itself. Become aware of what fear in your body feels like – maybe butterflies in your stomach; sweaty palms; needing to go to the toilet; or excessive worrying. As you become more adept at recognising fear, you will find that you are able to allow the *appropriate* amount of fear to be present in any situation, rather than 'old fear' memories overwhelming you. For specific phobias, behavioural psychology has proved to be very successful. This always includes taking that initial step towards the fear, rather than continuing to run away.

Listen to your apprehension or anxiety. It has something

of value for you to hear, even if it is simply that you hate spiders. If you cannot identify a reason for the fear, just allow it to be there anyway, for it's allotted time, exploring the associated thought patterns if you can.

Because the effect of fear is often to stop us doing what we want to do (for example, fear of embarrassing ourselves might stop us from going out socially), the more we are able to treat fear as a companion, rather than an enemy, the fewer battles we will have. We can be in charge of the fear, rather than the fear being in charge of us. You might like to use an affirmation such as 'Fear has a place in my life', 'I welcome the message my apprehensiveness brings to me', or 'I am no longer dominated by fear; I am in charge of my life'.

> Stephen heard of a promotion opportunity at work; he was keen to apply but was afraid that he would not be successful – he had applied twice before for promotion and both times was turned down. Nevertheless, he got the relevant forms, but found it hard to actually fill them in (particularly the section on why he would be good for this job!). He finally convinced himself that it would be silly to apply and that he was better off where he was. However, the day after the application deadline, Stephen felt lethargic and depressed, and wished that he had applied after all.

In this situation, the end result could have been different if Stephen had been able to monitor his thought processes and allow himself to feel the extent of his fear. He could have used affirmations such as 'I am good enough for this job', 'This job, or something even better, comes to me now with ease', or 'I deserve this opportunity' to help support him. By allowing himself to feel his fear, he would probably have felt very different after his application was in. Even if he did not receive the promotion, he could have felt proud of himself for overcoming his fear and doing his best to move on in his career.

Apathy

Again, apathy, or its associated feelings, can stop us from fully living our lives. Lack of motivation, lack of interest, a mediocre feeling about life, are all part of this feeling. Maybe you recognise feeling listless, or bored, or feeling there is a purposelessness to everything? Perhaps you feel powerless. Let yourself become familiar with how you feel, even if it is numbness, which is just as valid a feeling as any other! If this is the case, explore how you know you feel numb or blank – what does it feel like in your body? If you find that you are unable to identify any feelings, look to your behaviour to see where you might be covering things up behind a screen. You have to start your journey from where you are, and if you are behind a screen, unable to feel, then you can start exploring why you are behind the screen in the first place. What is it that prevents you from emerging from behind your screen?

Happiness

Happiness is not, of course, regarded as a negative emotion. However, it can be that we find it difficult to allow ourselves to feel happy; or it can be a way of covering up other, more negative, feelings that we would prefer not to have. Again, it helps to know the 'symptoms' of happiness in your body in order to be able to identify this feeling. Next time you feel good, try noticing what is happening in your body. Are you smiling, walking with a spring in your step, or having a warm feeling in your heart – do you feel loving? These are some of the ways that happiness makes itself known to us. If you apply the cluster exercise to happiness, look at the words you have written down – you may find you can identify contentment, or a feeling of peacefulness more easily as a result. Also notice the kinds of thoughts you are having. Become more and more familiar with feelings of happiness so that you can more easily welcome them into your life and use them in their rightful place.

Being in charge of your feelings

Sometimes, rather than finding it difficult to identify our feelings, we have no trouble knowing how we feel – it's feeling too much that is the issue! If you tend to be over-emotional, then the challenge is learning to contain your feelings appropriately. Once again, this means becoming more familiar with the quality of your feelings. As I mentioned in the section on fear, *you* are in charge of your feelings – and if you think or feel that this is not the case, then you need to begin to set some boundaries around your feelings, for instance by allocating them a time span. Use your thoughts to help you in this process, maybe by saying to yourself, 'I do not need to cry right now; I can be strong', or 'I contain my anger more and more easily'.

Often we have an emotion that we find comes more readily to the fore for us than others. For instance, many women find it relatively easy to cry, and will find themselves crying in a situation where it might be more appropriate to be angry. Many men find the opposite, where it is easier for them to express anger rather than sadness or hurt. With both sexes it is often easier to be fearful than to feel angry. Some people may find themselves being relentlessly 'upbeat' and 'chatty' as a way of avoiding other more uncomfortable feelings. If you find that this is the case for you, take charge of your feelings by being willing to explore the kinds of thoughts linked to this emotion and any other feelings that may be around. Later, when not so emotional, you may be able to understand why you were thinking those particular thoughts at that time. What this then requires is your willingness to be honest with yourself, to tell yourself the truth about what was really going on for you in that moment. You might choose to do the exercise in Chapter Four about storylines, dramas and themes.

Separating past feelings from the present

When we feel inordinately strongly about something, it is often the case that our current feelings are being heavily influenced by our past feelings about similar events, almost as if the feelings from the past are right here in the present. On the strength of these feelings, we may even feel transported back into the past, sometimes to the extent of feeling much younger again. When this is the case, being willing and able to feel these feelings from the past, whatever they are, frees us to move on in our lives.

These past feelings have become stuck in our bodies, unable to be expressed; but when they are released, a freedom comes which means that we have created a space where we can let go, move forward, and stop being hampered by the influence of past events in the present. To help in this process, a useful question to ask ourselves is, 'How old do I feel now?' Often our intuitive answer will tell us something about the origin of the feeling, which makes it easier to allow ourselves to express it, let it go, and move on.

Embracing our younger selves

Everyone has a younger aspect to themselves – we can think back to when we were 21, 16, 10, 5, maybe even younger. We can remember, to whatever extent, what we looked like, what we were doing, how we felt, what were our likes and dislikes. Being who you were at that age has contributed to who you are now, and having an understanding of that will contribute to your understanding of yourself now. Looking back with compassion and forgiveness at the person or child you once were, and seeing yourself and your behaviour from this perspective, can really help in accepting who and where you are today. Likewise, being willing to explore and accept how you might have felt when you were younger has a similar beneficial effect.

Your childhood did not necessarily just contain sadness, or any other 'negative' emotion – many of us have very happy memories of some delightful times in childhood. You may remember feeling mischievous, having lots of fun, being thrilled by new experiences – in other words, taking pleasure in exploring the world. So if you choose to connect with your past in this way, be open to experiencing the whole range of feelings, from happy to sad, from angry to excited!

Connecting with your younger self

To do this exercise, have some blank paper, and two different coloured pens to hand. Closing your eyes if it helps you to concentrate, imagine yourself when you were younger. Any age is fine, but to start with I suggest you bring to your mind's eye an image of when you were about five or six. If you have no memories of yourself at this time, then pick another age. Notice what you are wearing, and where you are. Are you alone? Do you have any idea of what your younger self might be thinking or feeling?

Now take some of your paper, and draw a picture of this little child, using the hand you don't usually write with, the non-dominant hand. Let yourself draw whatever comes to mind, and in whatever way – it may turn out like your mental image, or not – it doesn't matter. When you are finished, take some time to reflect on the picture and what it means to you. (If you are doing this with a partner, talk to each other about your pictures.) Also notice how you are feeling.

Next, take another sheet of paper and begin a conversation with your younger self. Using the hand you normally write with, take one of the pens and begin by saying hallo, or introduce yourself. Ask your younger self if they would like to talk to you. Then take the other pen in the other hand, and let your younger self communicate through your non-dominant hand whatever they want to say. Ask them questions such as:

What's your name? (especially if you had a different name when you were younger)

How old are you right now?

What do you like doing?

How are you feeling today?

What can I do for you?

How do you feel about your life? (you could choose a specific incident if you wish)

When communicating in this way, it is very important that you do your best to listen to your younger self. The most important gift you can give this part of you is your ability to listen and to love, without judgement. During an inner con-

HALLO LITTLE MARY – ARE YOU THERE?
Yes I'm sad
OH, WHY'S THAT?
Becas you're not paying me enough attention
WELL OK. HERE I AM NOW. WHAT WOULD YOU LIKE?
A soft cuddle
OK. HERE YOU ARE – HOW'S THAT?
I love it when you cuddle me
IS THERE ANYTHING ELSE I CAN DO FOR YOU RIGHT NOW?
CUP OF TEA!
OK!

mmm quiet + peaceful so sleepy
zzzz

I like being quiet when I feel quiet inside

versation like this, you can give yourself what you needed when you were younger, and therefore this process can be very helpful in your personal journey. Take your time – as with any new relationship, you will need to build up trust; *listening to and hearing* the younger you is very important.

This technique of writing with your other hand is very successful at allowing you to access this younger self. You can use this method whenever you wish to communicate with this part of you, for example, if you wish to know another opinion of what you are doing with your life, or how that part of you is feeling. Remember, this is not a separate person you are in touch with – it is simply another aspect of yourself, which will help you become more aware of who you are in the present.

When practising becoming more familiar with your feelings, use affirmations to help you along the way. Some have already been suggested; here are some others:

I find it easier and easier to feel my feelings

Feelings make me feel alive!

I am now in charge of my emotions

I choose to express my feelings when I wish

As I respect my feelings more, so too do others

I welcome the lessons my feelings have for me

I relax and allow myself to feel

Conclusion

Deeper awareness of my thoughts and feelings from using these techniques has been a very powerful influence in allowing me to make changes in life. Everything that I have written about I have practised, and do practise myself – this is how I have discovered so many ways to observe my thoughts and feelings, and how to change them! My journey has, at times, been challenging, but it has also been absolutely fascinating in the discoveries I have made, not only about myself, but also about others and how we all inter-relate as human beings. The ideas and exercises you have read are what contributed greatly to my recovery from bulimia and compulsive overeating. I also applied these principles to my pattern of only being attracted to men who were unavailable; this had caused me great unhappiness – but I was able to interrupt this pattern and am now happily married.

One of the most important ideas that I integrated into my life during this time was that I realised that I could choose how to respond to different circumstances in my life. These days it is easier and easier to choose to be happy. My tolerance level for struggle and pain has dropped, and I consequently put more energy into finding happiness wherever I am. This is not to say that there are not setbacks, or times when I feel very low, but rather that I can incorporate these into the richness of the patchwork quilt of my life. These hard times can be just as valuable as the more pleasant times, and work together to make life richer. Along the way, I have also learnt the importance of being me – and of being the best me I can! This is what I am most likely to be successful at, and to enjoy.

Remember, you are a unique and wonderful human being. No-one else could possibly do as good a job as you can at being you – so be you; discover and keep on discovering who you really are, and enjoy yourself while you are doing it!

Appendix A

*Life-affirming resources
for you and your world*

Living Well is owned and run by Jane Duncan and Philip Rogers. They give talks, run workshops and courses, and occasionally residential groups. They also offer a correspondence course based on this book. Audio tapes currently available are:

MAKING CHANGES – How to use positive affirmations even when you don't believe them by JANE DUNCAN, with music by Brian Boothby.

Side 1: Jane talks about the thinking behind the use of affirmations and how we can change our lives by catching our thoughts.

Side 2: Affirmations covering life, the body and health, love and intimacy, relationships, creativity, letting go/forgiveness and feelings.

Set to original music by Brian Boothby, Jane invites you to say the affirmations with her to help you change your life. Play this tape anywhere! Length: 60 minutes.

LIFE SUPPORTS YOU – Powerful visualisations for relaxing and releasing by JANE DUNCAN with music by Brian Boothby.

Side 1: White Light Meditation. Use light as a support, to help you feel safe, to feel that you belong, and to feel calmer.

Side 2: Taking Off Your Armour. Develop more satisfying relationships and begin to feel better about yourself by learning about your protective armour.

Length: 40 minutes.

THE FIVE MINUTE RELAXATION TAPE spoken by Philip Rogers with harp music by Brian Boothby.

Listening to Philip's calm and soothing voice, you are encouraged to simply take five minutes to relax your mind and body. No need to set aside half an hour any more – this tape can be used at any point during your day (except while driving) to help you release stress and invite calmness and peace of mind. Use on waking, going to sleep, travelling to work, during breaks or lunchtimes – any time you feel you need a breather, this tape will provide it. Length: 6 minutes per side.

THE BUSKER Brian Boothby.

Timeless tunes played on the Irish brass-strung harp. Chrome tape. Length: c. 45 minutes.

Jane and Philip also run a variety of groups and workshops. For full information on these, their tapes and other products, please contact them at Living Well, 27 Earl St, Oxford, OX2 0JA. Telephone 07050 074875 (mobile phone rates).

Appendix B: The Vocabulary of Feelings

From Beth Hedva, *Journey from betrayal to trust: A universal rite of passage*, published by Celestial Arts (1992).

STRONG

HAPPY	CARING	DEPRESSED
thrilled	tenderness toward	desolate
on cloud nine	affection for	dejected
ecstatic	captivated by	hopeless
overjoyed	attached to	alienated
excited	devoted to	depressed
elated	adoration	gloomy
sensational	loving	dismal
exhilarated	infatuated	bleak
fantastic	enamoured	in despair
terrific	cherish	empty
on top of the world	idolise	barren
turned on	worship	grieved
euphoric		grief
enthusiastic		despair
delighted		grim
marvellous		
great		

MODERATE

HAPPY	CARING	DEPRESSED
cheerful	caring	distressed
light-hearted	fond of	upset
happy	regard	downcast
serene	respectful	sorrowful
wonderful	admiration	demoralised
up	concern for	discouraged
aglow	hold dear	miserable
glowing	prize	pessimistic
in high spirits	taken with	tearful
jovial	turned on	weepy
riding high	trust	rotten
elevated	close	awful
neat		horrible
		terrible
		blue
		lost
		melancholy

MILD

HAPPY	CARING	DEPRESSED
glad	warm toward	unhappy
good	friendly	down
contented	like	low
satisfied	positive toward	bad
gratified		blah
pleasant		disappointed
pleased		sad
fine		glum

Appendix B: The vocabulary of feelings

STRONG

INADEQUATE	FEARFUL	CONFUSED
worthless	terrified	bewildered
good for nothing	frightened	puzzled
washed up	intimidated	baffled
powerless	horrified	perplexed
helpless	desperate	trapped
impotent	panicky	confounded
crippled	terror-stricken	in a dilemma
inferior	stage fright	befuddled
emasculated	dread	in a quandary
useless	vulnerable	full of questions
finished	paralysed	confused
like a failure		

MODERATE

inadequate	afraid	mixed-up
whipped	scared	disorganised
defeated	fearful	foggy
incompetent	apprehensive	troubled
inept	jumpy	adrift
overwhelmed	shaky	lost
ineffective	threatened	at loose ends
lacking	distrustful	going around in circles
deficient	risky	disconcerted
unable	alarmed	frustrated
incapable	butterflies	flustered
small	awkward	in a bind
insignificant	defensive	ambivalent
unfit		disturbed
unimportant		helpless
incomplete		embroiled
no good		
immobilised		

MILD

lacking confidence	nervous	uncertain
unsure of yourself	anxious	unsure
uncertain	unsure	bothered
weak	hesitant	uncomfortable
inefficient	timid	undecided
	shy	
	worried	
	uneasy	
	bashful	
	embarrassed	
	ill at ease	
	doubtful	
	jittery	
	on edge	
	uncomfortable	
	self-conscious	

Appendix B: The vocabulary of feelings

	HURT	ANGRY	LONELY	GUILT-SHAME
STRONG	crushed destroyed ruined degraded pain(ed) wounded devastated tortured disgraced humiliated anguished at the mercy of cast off forsaken rejected discarded	furious enraged seething outraged infuriated burned up pissed off fighting mad nauseated violent indignant hatred bitter galled vengeful hateful vicious	isolated abandoned all alone forsaken cut off	sick at heart unforgivable humiliated disgraced degraded horrible mortified exposed
MODERATE	hurt belittled shot down overlooked abused depreciated criticised defamed censured discredited disparaged laughed at maligned mistreated ridiculed devalued scorned mocked scoffed at used exploited debased slammed slandered impugned cheapened	resentful irritated hostile annoyed upset with agitated mad aggravated offended antagonistic exasperated belligerent mean vexed spiteful vindictive	lonely alienated estranged remote alone apart from others insulated from others	ashamed guilty remorseful crummy to blame lost face demeaned
MILD	put down neglected overlooked minimised let down unappreciated taken for granted	uptight disgusted bugged turned off put off miffed irked perturbed ticked off teed off chagrined cross dismayed impatient	left out excluded lonesome distant aloof	regretful wrong embarrassed at fault in error responsible for blew it goofed lament

Appendix C:
Some suggested further reading

Feelings
Goldbor Lerner – *The Dance of Anger*. Thorsons 1990.
Lindenfield – *Managing Anger*. Thorsons 1993.
Holden – *Living Wonderfully; a Joyful Guide to Conscious-Creative Living*. Thorsons 1994.
Weber – *Angry? Do You Mind If I Scream?* Health Communications, Inc 1991.
Jeffers – *Feel the Fear and Do It Anyway*. Arrow 1991.

Life and Death
Wilber – *Grace and Grit: spirituality and healing in the life and death of Treya Willam Kilber*. Shambhala 1991.
Levine – *Who Dies?* Gateway 1986.

Health
Shapiro – *Your Body Speaks Your Mind*. Piatkus 1996.
Hay – *You Can Heal Your Life*. Eden Grove 1984.
Dethlefsen – *The Healing Power of Illness*. Element 1990.

Spirituality
Hay – *The Power Is Within You*. Eden Grove 1991.
Gibran – *The Prophet*. Pan 1980.
Coit – *Listening – how to increase awareness of your inner guide*. Swan Publishing 1985.

Bloom – *First Steps: an introduction to spiritual practice*. Findhorn Press 1993.

Caddy – *Opening Doors Within*. Findhorn Press 1987.

Imagery

Glouberman – *Life Choices and Life Changes through Imagework*. Mandala 1989.

Gawain – *Creative Visualisation*. Bantam 1985.

Women

Northrup – *Women's Bodies, Women's Wisdom*. Piatkus 1995.

Claremont de Castillejo – *Knowing Woman*. Harper and Row 1973.

Dowling – *The Cinderella Complex; Women's Hidden Fear of Independence*. Fontana 1982.

Davis Kasl – *Women, Sex and Addiction*. Mandarin 1990.

Norwood – *Women Who Love Too Much*. Arrow 1986.

Men

Cohen – *Being A Man*. Routledge 1990.

Naifeh & White Smith – *Why Can't Men Open Up?* Sphere 1987.

Addictions

Roth – *Breaking Free from Compulsive Eating*. Signet 1984.

Beattie – *Co-Dependency No More*. Hazelden 1987.

Relationships

Cleese and Skynner – *Families and How To Survive Them*. Mandarin 1989.

Hendrix – *Getting the Love You Want*. Harper & Row 1988.

Younger Self books

Capacchione – *Recovery of Your Inner Child*. Simon & Schuster 1991.

Sark – *A Creative Companion*. Celestial Arts 1991.

Bradshaw – *Homecoming: Reclaiming and Championing Your Inner Child*. Piatkus 1991.

Miller – *The Drama of Being a Child*. Virago 1987.

Jungian

Johnson – *Inner Work*. Harper San Francisco 1986.

Johnson – *Owning Your Own Shadow*. Harper San Francisco 1993.

Meditation

Osho – *The Everyday Meditator*. Labyrinth Publishing 1989.

Long – *Meditation: A Foundation Course*. Barry Long Foundation 1986.

Others

Knight – *Talking to a Stranger: a consumer's guide to therapy*. Fontana 1986.

Bishop & Grunte – *How to Forgive When You Don't Know How*. Station Hill 1993.

Alexander – *The Natural Year: A seasonal guide to alternative health and beauty*. Bantam 1997.

Appendix D: Examples of Affirmative Notices

Appendix D: Examples of affirmative notices 125